Pizza

OVER 100 INNOVATIVE RECIPES FOR CRUSTS, SAUCES, AND TOPPINGS FOR EVERY PIZZA LOVER

Pippa Cuthbert and
Lindsay Cameron Wilson

Pizza

CompanionHouse Books™ is an imprint of Fox Chapel Publishers International Ltd.

Project Team
Vice President–Content: Christopher Reggio
Editor: Colleen Dorsey
Copy Editor: Laura Taylor
Design: Wendy Reynolds
Index: Jay Kreider
Recipe Photography: Stuart West

ISBN 978-1-62008-374-1

Library of Congress Control Number:2019945989

This book has been published with the intent to provide accurate and authoritative information in regard to the subject matter within. While every precaution has been taken in the preparation of this book, the author and publisher expressly disclaim any responsibility for any errors, omissions, or adverse effects arising from the use or application of the information contained herein.

Fox Chapel Publishing
903 Square Street
Mount Joy, PA 17552

Fox Chapel Publishers International Ltd.
7 Danefield Road, Selsey (Chichester)
West Sussex PO20 9DA, U.K.

www.facebook.com/companionhousebooks

We are always looking for talented authors. To submit an idea, please send a brief inquiry to acquisitions@foxchapelpublishing.com.

Printed and bound in China
22 21 20 19   2 4 6 8 10 9 7 5 3 1

Dedication

To our sisters: Anna, Sally, Lee, and Jessie.

Acknowledgments

Many thanks to Stuart West for his beautiful recipe
photographs and to all our friends and family who
contributed in countless ways to this book. And of course
to Books for Cooks, where all of this began.

The following images are credited to Shutterstock.com and their respective creators:
Front cover: Prostock-studio; 1: Africa Studio; 2–3: Tetiana Chernykova; 4–5: Natali Zakharova; 11: Vladimir
Volodin; 13: Billion Photos; 15: Luis Echeverri Urrea; 16: elizaveta66; 18: M. Unal Ozmen; 19: PARINYA ART;
23: id-art; 24: Alessio Orru; 26: beats1; 29: Bea Rue; 30: APIMGSTUDIO; 31: Sofia Iartseva; 32: Nata-Lia; 34:
MaraZe; 35: MARCELODLT; 37: Robyn Mackenzie; 41: AmyLv; 44: JeniFoto; 53: Diana Taliun; 55: zarzamora;
56: Nikolay Antonov; 60: Pixel-Shot; 61: Hong Vo; 67: Anatolii Riepin; 76: Angel Simon; 83: MRS. SUCHARUT
CHOUNYOO; 88: Tatyana Vyc; 96: Jiri Hera; 112: New Africa; 122: Imageman; 127: Binh Thanh Bui; 137:
kalavati; 148: Anatolii Riepin; 150: innakreativ; 151: Valery121283; 164: Tim UR; 169: robertsre; 171: Feng Yu;
189: Africa Studio

Contents

Introduction

Pizza is many things to many people. To the people of Naples, pizza is a way of life. There are more than 500 pizzerias amid the city's dusty churches and cramped dwellings. Within each pizzeria are veteran bakers standing before large, beehive-shaped wood-fired ovens. From these ovens come the traditional thin, puffy, charred crusts topped lightly with ingredients, such as the simple pizza Margherita, which is covered with tomatoes, olive oil, mozzarella, and basil. Legend has it that a chef in Naples created this colorfully patriotic pizza in 1889 when the Queen of Italy came to visit. Contrary to popular lore, however, pizza isn't an original Neapolitan idea; it's simply their interpretation of what the Greeks, the Romans, and undoubtedly the Arabs had been doing for centuries. Nevertheless, it is an interpretation that has clearly been successful.

To many Americans, pizza is something quite different. Italian immigrants brought Naples-style pizzas to America just before the turn of the twentieth century, but its popularity there didn't fully take off until the end of the Second World War, when US troops came home looking for the cheap, flavorful pizza they had tasted for the first time in Naples. According to Jeffrey Steingarten, the renowned American food writer and Neapolitan-American pizza aficionado, there are 61,269 pizzerias in America. Not all of these, however, uphold the traditions of Naples. Welcome the thick, deep-pan pizzas of Chicago. The garden-fresh, seasonal pizzas of California. The smoky, spicy pizzas of the Southwest. The thick and thin New York-style pizzas favored on the East Coast. There are even pizza fans who sincerely prefer the mass-produced, plastic-cheese-topped, pepperoni-studded, greasy creations from their local pizza chain. Yes, pizza has morphed in countless directions in America. It's fast food. It's street food. It's frozen. It's fresh. Some take pizzas seriously. Others down a slice while watching football.

But I'm not American. Nor is Pippa. America is just the perfect example of how a country can embrace a dish and shape it over time. Every country has its own variations, permutations, and interpretations of pizza. Some are good, others are shameful. The latter graced the dining room table of every primary school birthday party I ever attended. No, middle Americans are not alone. You know the kind of pizza I'm talking about—bland white crust, tasteless tomato sauce, and salty discs of pepperoni covered in a mound of "double" cheese—the rubbery stuff someone dared to call mozzarella. A little dough ball sat in the middle of these gargantuan pizzas. It kept the cardboard box from adhering to the sticky pizza during delivery.

As some say, you have to hit rock bottom before you can climb back up again. That's what we, two humble pizza lovers from separate ends of the globe, are here to do—to move pizza onwards and upwards, yet all the while keeping an eye on the past.

To us, pizza means Friday night. That was when imaginations ran wild and creative combinations began. It means trips to Italy. Memories of *pizza marinara* emerging from wood-fired ovens.

Folding it over and devouring it as fast as it was cooked. It means university. Cheap meals, quick nourishment, happy gatherings. It means barbecues, eating al fresco under the stars. Most of all, pizza means being given the opportunity to corral these memories into one collective book. Here you will find our favorite, eclectic, creative, and classic recipes from our repertoire. Some purists, like the members of the *Associazione Vera Pizza Napoletana*, who set out to defend the original Neapolitan pizza from imitations, wouldn't wholly approve. Our second chapter, aptly called Classics (see pages 56–75), is devoted entirely to the pizzas of southern Italy. It would pass, we think, with flying—red, white, and green—colors. The rest of the recipes veer, albeit thoughtfully, away. How can we not? I live in Canada, Pippa lives in New Zealand. We cook with what *we* have, with *our* seasons, and are inspired by unique flavor combinations and the incredible bounty of produce that is available to *us*. We're resourceful, much like the people of Naples. Ian Thomson, in Nikko Amandonico's *La Pizza*, explains: "During the hungry years of the Second World War, the city's seaside aquarium was ransacked by famished locals who boiled the tropical fish for a variety of unusual pizza and pasta dishes. Neapolitans give this resourcefulness a name—*l'arte di arrangiarsi*, the art of getting by."

We aren't starving, nor are we living in wartime. But we are blessed with *l'arte di arrangiarsi*. We love to experiment, to pair unexpected ingredients together, to fuse flavors. But you can't look forward without remembering the past. All of our recipes are based on the traditional pizza-making methods. Proper techniques are established. Flavor combinations are unique, but ingredients are pure. A wood-fired oven is encouraged. Of course we don't have one ourselves, but we'd really love it if we did. Dreaming aside, for the bulk of the home cooks out there, we've provided plenty of scope for experimentation. There are many sauces and pizza bases to choose from, depending on taste and time. The foundations are here, but as always, there is room to maneuver. Where some Neapolitans might scoff, the esteemed late English cookery writer Elizabeth David would hopefully approve. In 1954 *Italian Food* was first published in an attempt to provide a book for her English readers who had previously been "protected" from authentic versions of Italian cookery. "This is," wrote David in the 1963 introduction to the Penguin edition, "a book for those readers and cooks who prefer to know what the original dishes are supposed to be like, and to be given the option of making their own adaptations and alterations according to their tastes and circumstances."

Many years have passed since David wrote those words, but they still ring true today. No, the English are no longer making pizzas by topping crumpets with tomato purée and a slice of processed cheese, as they did to David's horror in the 1950s. But crumpet pizzas are a fine example of how individual interpretation free from any culinary tradition can be a recipe, for, well, disaster. If you set forth using *Pizza* as your guide, disaster will definitely be averted. Tradition will be upheld, but creativity encouraged. So go forth, we ask, with wild, leavened abandon.

Ingredients

PIZZA BASES

You can get great satisfaction from making your own pizza bases. Not only is the kneading process a great way to relieve stress, but the end result will also taste better than any store-bought alternative! It is important, when making bread, to understand your ingredients in order to achieve the best result possible within your limitations. Environmental factors such as temperature and humidity will play a part, as will the age of your flour, the hardness of your water, and the freshness of your yeast. One single bread-making experience will never be the same as the next. Understand your dough and follow your instincts. If it feels a little dry, then add more liquid early on; if it is too wet, then add a little more flour. Our recipes are not set in stone. With practice, you will become more aware of the signs to look out for and always end up with a soft and silky dough. If you are pressed for time, we do offer alternatives to making your own base (see page 18), which can make your cooking experience quick and very user-friendly without the extra flour mess!

MAKING PIZZA DOUGH

Mixing: This involves the mixing together of flour, water, and yeast—as simple as that. At this stage the gluten proteins begin to unfold and form water-protein complexes. Secondly, the yeast begins to feed on the sugars and starts the process of fermentation and the production of carbon dioxide. In some of our recipes we use the "sponge" method, which involves mixing up to half of the flour in with the yeast and water mixture. This can give a slightly more aerated end product due to the longer time of fermentation.

Kneading: This improves the aeration of the dough and furthers the development of the gluten. It is best done by hand if you prefer a product with larger air bubbles, but some bread machines and food

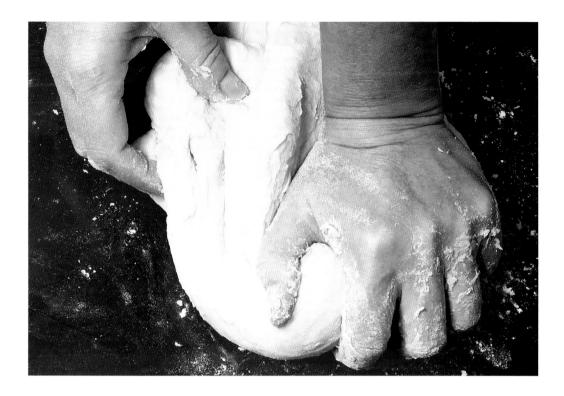

mixers these days do have dough hooks, which will result in a very fine, cake-like texture. Your technique for kneading will determine the final texture of your bread or base. Your dough is well kneaded when it takes on a silky, satiny appearance. Rich, buttery, or sweet doughs generally require longer kneading than others.

Rising (fermentation): This is the stage when the dough is set aside and covered with a clean tea towel in a warm place. The gluten development is still happening, but the main activity is the multiplication of yeast cells, which causes the dough to rise and expand. The yeast is producing more carbon dioxide, which in turn expands the air pockets, resulting in the final texture. The dough should approximately double in size, and then it is ready. At this stage, it is important to punch the dough back to release the pressure, shape it, and leave it for a further short rising. Then it is ready to be rolled out and topped.

Baking: When the dough is initially put in the oven, it will experience a sudden expansion, as the heat will cause a rapid production of carbon dioxide. When the interior of the dough reaches

about 140°F (60°C), the yeast cells will die and the rising will cease. The dough will then undergo a phase of browning, which will give the dough its crispy texture. The perfectly cooked dough should sound hollow when tapped.

FREEZING DOUGH

Your dough can be frozen as individual balls after the rising (fermentation) stage. Just knock the dough back, reshape into a ball, and place in a freezer bag. Remove the dough from the freezer about 6–8 hours before you need it. Leave it to defrost at room temperature. When you are ready, turn the plastic bag inside out and, using a floured hand, pull the dough from the bag. Knead the dough on a lightly floured surface for 5 minutes. Shape into a ball and leave for 20 minutes before rolling out.

FLOUR

There are two main types of wheat grown today, hard and soft, each with a characteristic kernel composition and each with its own particular culinary use. The wheat kernel will vary in "hardness," which is the measure of protein content and ultimately what determines the flour's gluten content. Hard flour contains large protein chunks and relatively little starch. As a result, this flour forms a strong gluten when mixed with water and is commonly used in bread making. In comparison, soft flours contain a higher starch content and consequently develop a weaker gluten. Soft flours are more commonly used for pasta and cakes where the texture is meant to be more tender and crumbly.

Gluten works rather like chewing gum. It is both plastic and elastic, that is, it will both change its shape under pressure and tend to reassume

its original shape when pressure is removed. Gluten stretches when worked and allows air to be incorporated and trapped, resulting in air bubbles. Bread making requires a hard flour in order for the carbon dioxide released by the yeast to be incorporated by the gluten, enabling the dough to rise. Pizza dough does not require the same level of rising action as a loaf of bread, and many people claim that a softer flour is actually better. The following is a guide to the different flours available and their uses.

Semolina: This is a coarse grain produced from the hardest kind of wheat grown today. It is predominantly used for very stiff doughs, particularly dried pastas. It is too hard for bread or pasta making, but can be added to pizza doughs for texture and crunch.

Hard flour: Grade 1 flour contains the highest gluten level and is generally used for bread making or pizzas. All-purpose flour can be used as well.

Soft flour: Grade 00 (*doppio zero*) flour is the finest grade and contains less gluten. It is useful for pasta making and baking. Soft flour can be used for pizza making, but make sure the package states that it is "panifiable."

ANCIENT GRAINS

Ancient grains, sometimes referred to as "heritage grains," are grains that have not been manipulated in a laboratory. Typically these grains are very simple and similar to a grain that was harvested hundreds of years ago, hence the name "ancient." The gluten and protein content is different than in other grains, which makes these grains much easier to digest. Common ancient grains include amaranth, barley, buckwheat, emmer, chia, farro, flax, Kamut, millet, oats, quinoa, rye, sorghum, spelt, teff, winter wheat, and wild rice. Corn, rice, and wheat are often classified as ancient grains as they too have ancient origins, but they have been modified from their original state. Some ancient grains, like buckwheat, chia, millet, and quinoa, are actually plants, but are grouped as grains because they can be used in the same way as cereal grains. Traditional grains, like wheat barley, farro, and spelt, are grasses. Some contain gluten and some do not. Oats, sorghum, and teff are gluten-free grains. The following grains and nut flours are some of the other "flours" we like to use in pizza making. Feel free to play with flours—substitute and experiment. Your results will depend on factors like the environment in which you live, the quality of your ingredients, and the heat of your oven. Have fun with it.

Buckwheat: Buckwheat dates back thousands of years to Siberia, the Himalayan Mountains, and Manchuria, areas where plants thrived and grew quickly in inferior soil and cool climates. It still thrives in similar conditions today, primarily in China, Australia, and Canada. The name buckwheat is misleading; buckwheat is a pseudo grain and is related to rhubarb! Buckwheat is gluten free, high in complex carbohydrates, and considered a complete protein. It can be purchased as kasha (roasted kernels), as groats (unroasted flakes or puffs), and as flour.

Spelt: Spelt is a type of grain that is strongly related to wheat. Spelt flour has fewer calories than wheat flour and is slightly higher in protein content, although it does contain some gluten. Spelt has a nutty, slightly sweet flavor.

Quinoa: Quinoa—a pseudo grain—is a seed from a plant related to spinach. Although quinoa was one of the foods worshipped by the Incas, it has experienced a renaissance relatively recently, mainly for its superfood status. Quinoa is high in protein, vitamins, and

minerals, and is gluten free, fulfilling many vegan, gluten-free, and healthy diet requirements.

Whole wheat: Also known as "wholemeal," whole wheat flour is made by grinding whole grains of wheat (with the bran and germ still intact) into flour. Whole wheat flours can vary in color; white whole wheat is made from hard white spring wheat, while traditional whole wheat is milled from red wheat. Whole wheat is high in protein and makes for a nutritious pizza dough. Try playing with the ratio of whole wheat and white flour in our pizza base recipes. Soon you'll find the combination you like best.

Nut flours: Also known as "nut meals," nut flours are not in fact flours but rather blanched and ground nuts. Compared to traditional gluten-free flours like rice, potato starches, or tapioca, nut flours have more protein and healthy fats that soften pizza dough and baked goods. They're also high in fiber and flavor (we love the sweetness of coconut flour in our cauliflower pizza, page 54). Once opened, transfer nut flours to an airtight container and store in the refrigerator or freezer.

Teff: The smallest of the grains, teff is of African origin, is gluten free, and is packed with protein. Teff is too small to be hulled, so it is primarily cooked in its whole seed form or ground into flour (teff flour is the main ingredient in injera, an Ethiopian flat bread). Its unique flavor tastes, some say, like hazelnuts or molasses. Either way, teff is bold; start by using it in combination with other flours.

YEAST

Yeasts are a group of single-celled fungi, about 160 different species of which are known. It is one species in particular, *Saccharomyces cerevisiae* or "brewer's sugar fungus," that is good for brewing and baking. Yeast gives off a characteristic flavor and smell; it leavens bread and converts the grain carbohydrates into alcohol and carbon dioxide. When we buy yeast, it is live but inactive. With a little warmth and the addition of some water, it is activated and releases the gas, carbon dioxide, that will raise the dough. The activity ceases only when the dough is placed in the oven and the yeast is killed by extreme heat.

Fresh yeast: This should be putty-like in color and texture; it should look firm and moist and feel cool to the touch. If it is dry, dark,

and crumbly, it may be stale or not live. Fresh yeast can be bought for a pittance from many supermarkets that have a bakery on site or from your local bakery. Keep fresh yeast in an airtight container in the fridge for up to 3 days. Alternatively, divide the yeast into ½ oz. or 1 oz. (15g or 30g) portions and freeze for up to 3 months. Always defrost your yeast thoroughly at room temperature or in the fridge before use.

To use: Using a spoon, crumble the fresh yeast into a small glass bowl and add about a quarter of the required amount of water as specified in the recipe to it. Use the back of the spoon to cream the yeast until it dissolves in the water and forms a smooth, blended paste. Stir in the remaining water. The yeast mixture is now ready to be added to the flour.

Dried granular yeast: This is usually bought in jars or cans from the supermarket. Dried yeast can be reconstituted with a little lukewarm water and will give exactly the same result as fresh yeast. Store it in an airtight container, and keep an eye on the expiration date. If it doesn't produce a frothy head when reconstituted with water, it is not viable.

To use: Sprinkle dried granular yeast into a small glass bowl containing the quantity of lukewarm water specified in the recipe. Leave to dissolve for 5–10 minutes. Once the yeast has dissolved, stir the mixture with a wooden spoon. The yeast mixture is now ready to be added to the flour. Continue as instructed in the recipe.

Dried easy-blend yeast: This is the easiest of yeasts to use as it is just added to the flour, with the water added separately. Again, the end product will be just as superior as using fresh or granular yeast. Always check the expiration date to ensure freshness.

To use: Sprinkle dried easy-blend yeast directly onto the flour. The yeast will activate once the liquid has been added. Continue as instructed in the recipe. Easy-blend yeast cannot be used for the "sponge" method (see page 36).

Notes
- ½ oz. (15g) fresh yeast = 2 tsp dried granular yeast = 2 tsp dried easy-blend yeast
- In the recipes, we have used dried granular yeast, and the method has been written to reflect this. If you want to use other types of yeast when making the recipes, refer back to these pages.

OLIVE OIL

We've used extra virgin olive oil in our recipes. Olive oils vary considerably in taste and strength. Choose one with a flavor you like. In some cases, we use infused olive oils, such as chili or basil oil.

Infused oils: You can buy these or make your own. To infuse oils, first wash and dry your chosen herb or spice and lightly bruise to release the flavor. Place the herbs or spices in a clean, sterilized jar or bottle and cover with warmed oil. Seal tightly and leave in a cool, dark place to infuse for about 2 weeks. Leave the herbs and spices in if you want a stronger flavor or a decorative look; otherwise strain. Use the oils within 2 months of initial bottling. Some suggested flavorings are basil, chili, rosemary, thyme, tarragon, cardamom, star anise, or cloves.

PIZZA BASE ALTERNATIVES

Pita bread: Use pita breads to make mini or individual pizzas, which are great for kids. Let them top their own and experiment with the ingredients.

Tortillas: These make a thin and crispy base. They can also be cooked in a frying pan and even topped with a second tortilla to make a quesadilla. Great served as a quick finger-food snack chopped into wedges.

Naan bread: Choose an Indian-inspired topping, such as spinach and paneer cheese, and finish it off with an authentic naan bread base. This is a breadier alternative to tortillas.

Puff pastry: It's hard to say whether making a pizza with puff pastry is cheating or not. Most of us would call this a tart, but it's basically the same concept and is a quick and easy alternative if you buy ready-rolled sheets.

Bought bases: Bought pizza bases come in many shapes and forms and are available from all good supermarkets. Try frozen, vacuum-packed, or ready-rolled bases from the frozen section. Some supermarkets or delicatessens may also sell frozen balls of pizza dough, which just require defrosting and shaping. Alternatively, get friendly with your local Italian restaurant—they may sell you frozen balls of dough.

TOMATOES

There are more than 5,000 varieties of tomato in the world today, from yellow cherry tomatoes and green plum tomatoes to red beef tomatoes! It was in Naples that tomatoes transformed the original white pizza into the red, tomato-topped variety we know today. Italian cooking without the tomato would truly be unthinkable. Tomatoes can be bought in many varieties: fresh, canned, puréed, sun-dried, and semi-dried are all readily available. Tomatoes are made up of about 94 percent water and must always be well drained, whether fresh or canned, in order to avoid a soggy pizza.

Canned tomatoes: These are scalded, peeled, and slightly salted before being canned. Canned tomatoes are a very popular choice for pizza makers today and are of equal quality to the fresh variety. In many cases it is the superior, unblemished tomatoes that are sent away for canning, when the not-so-perfect tomatoes are left behind for fresh sale.

Tomato purée: Many professional pizza makers steer clear of tomato purée, arguing that it tends to dull the other flavors, making all pizzas taste the same. We're not sure if this is truly the case, and it is certainly a useful ingredient if you want to assemble a pizza in a hurry.

CHEESES

Mozzarella

Mozzarella di bufala is the original mozzarella and is delicious served as is. It is sweet in flavor and soft in texture but does not melt as well as cow's mozzarella. Cow's milk mozzarella is the one to use for cooking. It has a very mild, creamy, and faintly sour flavor and melts beautifully, making it ideal for pizzas. Mozzarella can also be made with goat's milk, which is a little sharper in taste and is not such a popular choice.

Mozzarella is produced as a semi-soft, fresh cheese or a firm block of cheese made with low- or non-fat milk. The fresh cheese is the ultimate choice for home-made pizzas, but it is important to make sure you drain and dry it well to remove as much excess moisture as possible. Fresh mozzarella balls are usually packaged in water or, alternatively, brine or whey, to preserve freshness. Fresh mozzarella is mild in flavor, soft, and very pliable. The longer mozzarella ages, the softer and sourer it becomes. In all our recipes, we have used fresh mozzarella balls unless otherwise specified.

Mozzarella can also be found in other forms:

Block mozzarella: Block mozzarella is lower in moisture than fresh mozzarella and is often the preferred choice for many commercial pizza makers. In America as many as 90 percent of all commercial pizza makers will use block mozzarella. It is lower in fat and consequently not as flavorful as fresh mozzarella.

Bocconcini: These are small mozzarella balls usually about 1" (2.5cm) in diameter.

Mozzarella affumicata: *Affumicato* means smoked in Italian. This cheese is lightly smoked over wood chips and is darker in color than normal mozzarella.

Mozzarella scamorza: This mozzarella has been heavily smoked, usually over pecan shells, and is much darker in color and denser in texture.

Mozzarella pearls: Tiny balls of mozzarella, which are about ⅝" (1.5cm) in diameter. They are available from some supermarkets, but if you can't find them, then a large mozzarella ball cut into cubes does exactly the same thing.

Mozzarella can be wrapped in plastic food wrap and frozen for up to 3 months. Frozen mozzarella does decrease in flavor and may become moister in texture. Before serving or cooking, allow the cheese to defrost in the fridge before removing and warming to room temperature. Fresh mozzarella usually keeps for up to 2 weeks in the fridge.

Parmesan

When buying Parmesan cheese, always look for the words *Parmigiano reggiano* for authenticity and quality. Never buy pre-grated or shaved Parmesan in tubs. It is important to keep your Parmesan from drying out, so always buy a freshly cut piece and grate only when needed. Parmesan cheese is rich and round in flavor and has the ability to melt with heat and become inseparable from the ingredients to which it is joined. To store your Parmesan for longer than 2–3 weeks, divide it into pieces, each with a piece of rind still attached, and wrap tightly in greaseproof paper, then in heavy duty aluminum foil. Store on the bottom shelf of the fridge.

Pecorino

The Italian word for sheep is *pecora*, hence all cheese made from sheep's milk is called pecorino. There are dozens of pecorinos available: some are soft and fresh, while others are crumbly and sharp, more like a Parmesan.

Fontina

Fontina is a semi-hard cheese with a creamy texture and subtle nutty flavor. It is a very useful cheese for cooking as it has good melting properties, making it a popular choice in fondues and pizzas. Fontina is made from unpasteurized cow's milk from the grazing cows of the Val d'Aosta alpine region of Italy.

Ricotta

The word *ricotta* literally means "recooked" in Italian. It is made from the whey of other cheeses that is cooked again to make a milky white, soft, granular, and mild-tasting cheese. Ricotta does not melt.

Gruyère

Gruyère is a firm cheese with a nutty flavor. It works best when finely grated.

Asiago

A semi-firm to hard Italian cheese with a nutty, sharp flavor that is mainly used for grating. Asiago was traditionally made with sheep's milk, but it is now more commonly made with cow's milk.

Havarti

Havarti is a mild, semi-soft Danish cheese with small, irregular holes.

Monterey Jack

Monterey Jack is a type of Cheddar-style cheese first made in California using pasteurized cow's milk. It is commonly sold by itself, or mixed with Colby cheese to make a marbled cheese known as Colby-Jack (or Co-Jack).

Cheddar
Choose a mature Cheddar for the best flavor and always grate for use on pizza to get a more even melt.

Provolone
This is a southern Italian cheese that is pale yellow in color, with a smooth texture. Milder, fresh provolone can be eaten on its own, although once aged it is generally used in cooking.

Gorgonzola
Gorgonzola is a mild and creamy blue-veined cheese. Choose dolcelatte if you prefer a creamier, milder soft blue cheese.

Taleggio
Taleggio is a semi-soft cheese made from whole cow's milk. Its flavor can range from mild to pungent, depending on its age. When young,

the color of taleggio is pale yellow. As it ages, it darkens to deep yellow and becomes rather runny. Taleggio is sold in blocks and is covered either with a wax coating or a thin mold.

Mascarpone

Mascarpone is a soft, unripened cheese that belongs to the cream cheese family. It comes from northern Italy and is a thick, rich, sweet, velvety, ivory-colored cheese produced from cow's milk that has the texture of sour cream. It is sold in plastic tubs and can be found in most delicatessens and good supermarkets.

Halloumi

Halloumi is a semi-hard, unripened, brined cheese made from a mixture of goat's and sheep's milks, and sometimes also cow's milk. Halloumi has a high melting point, so it can be easily fried or grilled without losing its shape.

Vegan cheeses

Cheese is traditionally a dairy product, meaning it is derived from milk (cow, goat, sheep, or buffalo). Vegan cheese, on the other hand, is entirely plant based. Vegan cheese is aimed at vegans or other people wanting to avoid animal products. Vegan cheese is predominantly made from soy protein, seeds (such as sesame and sunflower), nuts (such as cashew, pine nut, and almonds), or solidified vegetable oil.

CURED MEATS

Prosciutto

Prosciutto is the pig's hind thigh or ham that has been salted and air-dried. The salt draws off the meat's excess water, thus curing and preserving it. A true prosciutto is never smoked. When served, it should always be thinly sliced and used as soon as possible. If you are not consuming it immediately, then each slice or each single

layer of slices must be covered with greaseproof paper or plastic wrap (clingfilm) then wrapped in aluminum foil. Prosciutto is delicious eaten as it is or cooked on pizzas. It can be quite salty, so do not add extra salt unless needed.

Pancetta

Pancetta is from the pig's belly and is the Italian equivalent of bacon. Pancetta can be bought sliced or cubed and is more tender and considerably less salty than prosciutto. It can also be eaten raw or cooked. Pancetta is rarely ever smoked except in a few areas of northern Italy.

Salami

Salami is the generic term for cured and fermented meat (usually pork or beef) that is typically flavored with spices such as black pepper, fennel, chili, or paprika. The meat mixture is ground and stuffed into casings, then hung to dry, either in hot or cool air, until the sausages have reduced in weight by at least half. Some salamis or cured sausages will also be smoked. Examples of common salamis and cured sausages are Napoli, Milano, Genoa, chorizo, and pepperoni.

Mortadella

Mortadella can be used sliced or diced on pizzas. It is made from the lean shoulder and neck meat from carefully selected pigs and is then studded with the creamy fat from other parts of the pig. Mortadella is often flavored with a blend of spices and condiments that varies from producer to producer.

Bresaola

Bresaola is very thinly sliced, cured and air-dried lean beef. It is gently spiced to develop its rich and aromatic flavor.

Equipment

COOKING METHODS

Wood-fired oven

This is an essential factor in the creation of the true Neapolitan pizza. The design of the traditional wood-fired pizza oven is more than 2,000 years old. These ovens are dome-shaped, made from brick or clay, and the roof is heated by direct contact with the flames from the burning wood below. The dome shape then causes the heat to be reflected back down to the base of the oven.

In a well-used oven (such as those in many pizzerias in Naples), the fire will never go out completely—even when there are no pizzas in the oven. The flames will die right down and just embers will be left burning so the oven can be bought back up to temperature at a much faster rate. A pizza oven will reach about 750°F (400°C), at which temperature a pizza will cook in about a minute and a half. If you are lucky enough to have a wood-fired oven, the woods of choice are cherry or olive wood, as they don't smoke as much as other woods. Make sure you also invest in a long pizza paddle to get your pizzas in and out of the deep oven.

Wood-fired ovens are becoming more and more popular as an outside alternative to a grill/barbecue. They are used to cook a wide variety of foods, not just pizzas. Whole large roasts and loaves of bread can be successfully cooked in them as well as semi-dried tomatoes, zucchini (courgettes), and other vegetables.

Electric/gas oven

For a while, electric ovens were beginning to replace the traditional wood-fired oven in many pizzerias around the world. It seems today that the wood-fired oven may be making a comeback in most pizzerias, but for many of us, an electric or gas oven is still the main

oven of choice. With an electric oven, we have a lot more control over temperature, and this makes it more suited to most domestic homes. Although the flavor and smell may not be quite as authentic as that of a wood-fired oven, the pizza that you will produce can still be of top quality. It may be worth investing in a pizza stone if you are planning on doing some serious pizza making at home (see below). All our recipes are tested in fan-assisted (or convection) ovens, which produce a crisper, golden crust.

Pizza stone

A pizza stone will transform your electric or gas oven into the modern equivalent of the clay and brick ovens used by traditional pizza bakers. Cooking pizzas on a stone gives them a crispness that cannot otherwise be achieved from an oven. Most pizza stones have been fired at temperatures in excess of 2,000°F (1,100°C). This enables them to give a very dry heat that is also evenly distributed, eliminating any hot spots and giving a consistent browning to your pizza. Pizza stones are suitable for use in both gas or electric ovens. Try serving your pizza directly on the stone and it will stay hot right through until the last slice. It is important to always heat your pizza stone first so it can absorb the heat of the oven. You will need a pizza paddle (see page 31), or use our parchment paper technique (see page 32) to transfer your topped pizza quickly onto the stone without losing too much heat. Alternatively, you will need to work very quickly to assemble your topping. Sprinkle a little flour on the pizza stone first to keep it from sticking. Be very careful when handling the stone, as it gets very hot and will remain hot for a long time.

In our recipes, we have said to use a baking sheet as not everyone will have a pizza stone, but if you do have one, use it!

Grill

Cooking pizza on a grill/barbecue is a great way to impress your guests. It requires no special skills, just the flick of the switch or some burning coals. It's a good idea to keep a supply of frozen pizza dough balls in the freezer for those spontaneous summer evenings. Just defrost the dough (see page 12), roll it out, and within minutes you can have a crisp, slightly charred crust with your chosen topping. Some topping ingredients, such as bunches of cherry tomatoes or

grilled eggplants (aubergines), are best cooked separately. Let the cheese melt on the base and throw the extra topping on—presto!

OTHER EQUIPMENT

Pizza paddle
If you own a wood-fired oven or a pizza stone, then a pizza paddle is definitely worth investing in. Always lightly flour it before setting the dough on it so that the pizza can easily be transferred to the oven or onto the pizza stone.

Thermometer
If you are lucky enough to own a wood-fired oven, then a good thermometer is essential in order to judge the inside temperature of the oven. Choose one that reaches a temperature of at least 750°F (400°C).

Pizza plates

If you don't have a pizza stone on which to serve your pizza, then you will need to buy a few flat, round plates for serving. Alternatively, large chopping boards will suffice.

Pizza cutter

A pizza cutter definitely speeds up the cutting process.

Baking parchment

Baking parchment can be very useful to help transfer your topped pizza onto your baking sheet or pizza stone. Make sure the paper is lightly floured, and roll out your pizza dough on it just as you would on any other surface. Slide the paper and dough onto the pizza stone or baking sheet and leave the paper there during cooking.

Ladle

A ladle is useful for transferring sauce from the bowl to the pizza base. Then use the base of the ladle to distribute the sauce around the base, ensuring you leave a ½"–¾" (1–2cm) border. Most of our pizzas call for 4 fl. oz. (125ml) of sauce, so try buying a ladle that fits this volume exactly.

RECIPE INFORMATION

- All pizza recipes make 1 pizza unless otherwise specified and generally serve 1–2 people.
- For all our recipes, we have given our preferred choice of base and sauce. These are not set in stone; it is important to mix and match and experiment with different flavor combinations.
- All our recipes have been tested in a fan-assisted (convection) oven. **If you are using a conventional oven, then increase our recommended cooking temperature of 425°F/220°C/gas mark 7 to 475°F/240°C/gas mark 9.** All ovens vary in performance, so always check that your pizza is cooked to the desired crispness before serving.
- Keep your pizza toppings simple and the result will always be better.
- Unless otherwise stated, pizzas should always be served straight from the oven while the base is still crispy.
- Always use floured work surfaces and hands when working with pizza bases.
- In all our recipes, we have used fresh mozzarella unless otherwise specified.
- Remember, plain flour is also known as all-purpose flour.

REMEMBER:
The recipe cook times and temperatures given are for fan-assisted (convection) ovens. If you are using a conventional oven, then increase the recommended cooking temperature of 425°F/220°C/gas mark 7 to 475°F/240°C/gas mark 9. All ovens vary, so always check that your pizza is cooked!

Bases and breads

Many say there is nothing better than the thin, puffy crust of a Neapolitan pizza. It is a beautiful thing, we know. But it's good to stretch the comfort zone. Try something new. Experiment. Break free!

Pizza lovers in Chicago have certainly broken free. The cold, windy winters call for thick, deep crusts with lots of toppings. Wet, substantial toppings and a thick layer of cheese call for a thick crust. The heat of the oven melds everything into the crust, fusing the two together into one comforting mass. The weather calls for it, the body needs it.

Then there are those looking for speed. That's where our no-rise crusts come in. And for those with problems with gluten? There is something for them as well. Either way, simply compile, mix, roll, and top. It's as simple as that. Making dough is perhaps the easiest experiment in breaking free imaginable.

Don't forget the sweet. Our honey-infused, saffron-scented crust will make you smile. Topped with sweet pears and walnuts, caramelized apples, or simply served neat, dabbling in sweet territory will bring you, well, sweet success.

This dough uses the "sponge" method—some of the flour is added to the water and yeast, and the resulting "sponge" is allowed to rest before the remaining flour is mixed in.

Crispy pizza base

PERFECTION | Makes 4 x 10"–12" (25–30cm) pizzas

- 4 tsp dried granular yeast
- 10 fl. oz. (300ml) lukewarm water
- 1 lb. 2 oz. (500g) plain flour
- 1 tsp salt

Sprinkle the yeast into 3½ fl. oz. (100ml) of the water. Leave to dissolve for 5–10 minutes. Add about 2 Tbsp of the flour and mix to a smooth paste, then stir in the remaining water. Cover and leave the yeast mixture for about 30 minutes or until it is bubbling and foamy.

Combine the flour (reserve 2 Tbsp for kneading) and salt in a large bowl and make a well in the center. Pour in the yeast liquid. Using a wooden spoon, work the ingredients together by pulling the flour into the liquid until it comes together. Use your hands to transfer the mixture to a lightly floured surface. Knead the dough for 10 minutes or until it is smooth and elastic. Form the dough into a round loaf. Leave to rise under a clean tea towel for about 1½–2 hours or until doubled in size.

Punch down the dough and knead for a couple of minutes. Divide into four balls. Press each dough ball out flat and, using a floured rolling pin, shape into a 10"–12" (25–30cm) diameter circle. Using your knuckles, press just inside the edges to raise them slightly. Leave to rest for 10–15 minutes. Preheat oven to 425°F/220°C/gas mark 7.

Add your toppings. Cook in the middle of the oven for 10–12 minutes (unless otherwise instructed depending on the toppings) or until crispy and golden and the base is cooked.

Quick scone base

SIMPLICITY | Makes 1 x 10" (25cm) pizza

- 9 oz. (250g) plain flour or 00 flour
- 1 tsp baking powder
- 1 pinch salt
- 1¼ oz. (30g) butter (at room temperature), cut into cubes
- 7–9 fl. oz. (200ml) milk

Preheat the oven to 400°F/200°C/gas mark 6. Sift and combine the flour, baking powder, and salt in a large bowl. Add the cubes of butter and lightly rub into the flour until the mixture resembles the texture of breadcrumbs. Add the milk to the rubbed mixture and stir with a palette knife or metal spoon until it begins to come together. Finish it off with your hands—it should be soft but not sticky (if the dough seems too dry, add a little more milk, a teaspoon at a time). The dough should come together and leave the sides of the bowl clean.

Shape the dough into a ball with your hands and transfer it to a lightly floured surface. Flour a rolling pin and roll the dough out to about ½" (1cm) thick and 10" (25cm) in diameter.

Place the round on a lightly floured baking sheet and top as required. Cook in the middle of the preheated oven for 12–18 minutes, depending on the topping, or until cooked and golden.

Every so often the need strikes for a thick, luscious crust to sink your teeth into. This recipe will satisfy that need!

Thick-crust pizza base/ calzone dough

TENDER | Makes 4 x 12" (30cm) pizzas or 6 x 8"–10" (20–25cm) calzoni

- 2 Tbsp dried granular yeast
- 18 fl. oz. (500ml) lukewarm water
- 1 lb. 10 oz. (750g) plain flour
- 3 oz. (80g) cornmeal or polenta
- 2 tsp salt
- 4 fl. oz. (125ml) olive oil

Sprinkle the dried granular yeast into the water. Leave to dissolve for 5–10 minutes.

Combine the flour, cornmeal, and salt in a large mixing bowl. Make a well in the center and slowly add olive oil and yeast mixture. Stir with a wooden spoon until the mixture is roughly combined. It will be quite moist.

Lightly flour a work surface and tip out the dough. Knead for 8–10 minutes until smooth and elastic. Place the dough in a large, clean, oiled bowl, cover, and leave to rise for 1 hour or until doubled in size.

Preheat the oven to 425°F/220°C/gas mark 7. Knead the dough again a few times, then divide it into four equal parts to make four 12" (30cm) pizzas, or six equal parts to make six 8"–10" (20–25cm) calzoni. Place on a lightly floured baking sheet.

Add your toppings and cook in the middle of the preheated oven for 14–16 minutes or until crispy and golden and the base sounds hollow when tapped.

Ancient grains are referred to as such because they have remained largely unchanged for hundreds or even thousands of years. Quinoa gives this pizza base texture and character; choose white, red, or black quinoa depending on what is available.

Ancient spelt and quinoa pizza base

TEXTURAL, WHOLESOME, RUSTIC | Makes 3 x 12" (30cm) pizzas

- 1¾ oz. (50g) quinoa (choose red, white, or black)
- 4 tsp dried granular yeast
- 5 fl. oz. (150ml) lukewarm water
- 11½ oz. (325g) spelt flour
- 1 tsp fine salt
- 2 Tbsp extra virgin olive oil

Place the quinoa in a bowl and cover with ¼ cup (60ml) cold water. Leave to absorb for 4–6 hours. Drain off any excess water (it will still be wet).

Sprinkle the dried yeast into the water. Leave to dissolve for 5–10 minutes.

Combine the flour, salt, and quinoa in a large mixing bowl. Make a well in the center and slowly add the olive oil and yeast mixture. Stir with a wooden spoon until the mixture is roughly combined.

Transfer the dough onto a lightly floured work surface and knead for 8–10 minutes until smooth. Place the dough in a large, clean, lightly oiled bowl. Cover and leave to rise for 60–90 minutes or until doubled in size.

Preheat the oven to 425°F/220°C/gas mark 7. Knead the dough again a few times, then divide into three equal portions. Roll the portions on a lightly floured surface to about ¹⁄₁₆" (2mm) thick.

Add toppings and cook in the preheated oven for 10–12 minutes or until the crust is golden and the cheese is bubbling.

The ketogenic diet is a high-fat, adequate protein, low-carbohydrate diet that forces the body to burn fats rather than carbohydrates. The key to this keto-friendly pizza base is to pre-bake the base before topping it and eating it straight from the oven!

Keto-friendly pizza base

LOW-CARB | Makes 1 x 12" (30cm) pizza

- 5 ¼ oz. (150g) almond meal
- ½ tsp fine salt
- 2 oz. (50g) finely grated Parmesan cheese
- ½ tsp dried oregano (optional)
- 3 Tbsp coconut oil
- 1 egg, lightly beaten

Preheat the oven to 350°F/180°C/gas mark 4.

Put the almond meal, salt, cheese, and oregano in a large bowl. Gently combine the coconut oil and egg. Make a well in the center of the dry ingredients and add the egg mixture. Stir well until the mixture comes together in a ball.

Roll the ball out between two sheets of baking parchment to 12" (30cm) in diameter, tidying the edges as you go to make it as round as possible. Place on a pizza tray or baking tray. Remove the top sheet of baking parchment and bake in the preheated oven for 8–10 minutes. Remove from the oven and top as desired before returning to the oven. Cook for 8–10 more minutes or until the crust is golden and the cheese is bubbling. Serve immediately.

These little morsels make a great party canapé. Top them with whatever you like or keep them plain to dip into hummus or guacamole.

Pizza bites

INSPIRATIONAL | Makes 20–24

- 1 x 12" (30cm) Crispy pizza base (see page 36)
- 4 Tbsp Cilantro (coriander) pesto (see page 180)
- 4 Tbsp cream cheese
- 2 green (spring) onions, sliced
- Sweet chili sauce, to serve
- Cilantro leaves (coriander), to serve

Preheat the oven to 425°F/220°C/gas mark 7.

Prepare the pizza dough and roll it out to a 12" (30cm) round as you would if making one round pizza. Using a small metal pastry cutter, cut as many rounds from the dough as possible. Carefully transfer the rounds to a lightly floured baking sheet.

Prick each round once or twice with a fork. Top each round with about ½ tsp Cilantro (coriander) pesto and ½ tsp cream cheese. Sprinkle on 2–3 slices of green (spring) onion and cook in the middle of the preheated oven for 6–8 minutes or until golden and crisp. Serve hot, warm, or cold topped with sweet chili sauce and cilantro (coriander).

This base is very similar in flavor and texture to our Quick scone base (see page 37), but the addition of rice flour makes it friendlier to those with wheat allergies.

Gluten-free quick pizza base

SOFT | Makes 2 x 12" (30cm) thin crusts

- 6 oz. (175g) brown or white rice flour
- 1 Tbsp extra-fine (caster) sugar
- ½ tsp baking soda (bicarbonate of soda)
- ½ tsp salt
- 8 fl. oz. (225ml) plain yogurt

Preheat the oven to 350°F/180°C/gas mark 4.

Combine the flour, sugar, baking soda (bicarbonate of soda), and salt in a large bowl. Add the yogurt and stir until roughly combined. Turn the dough onto a floured surface and knead for 1 minute, or until it comes together into a smooth ball. Form into two balls with your hands and transfer to a lightly floured surface. Flour a rolling pin and roll the dough to about ½" (1cm) thick and 10" (25cm) in diameter. Place onto a lightly floured baking sheet and top as required. Cook in the middle of the preheated oven for 12–15 minutes or until cooked and golden.

All that's needed to make this pizza is a grill with a lid, clear skies, and appetites.

Grilled pizza base

SMOKY | Makes 6 x 8" (20cm) pizzas

› 2 tsp dried granular
  yeast
› 10 fl. oz. (275ml)
  lukewarm water
› About 1 lb. 2 oz. (500g)
  plain flour
› 2 tsp salt
› 2½ fl. oz. (75ml) olive oil,
  plus extra for brushing

Sprinkle the yeast into the water. Leave to dissolve for 5–10 minutes. Combine the flour and salt in a large bowl. Slowly add the yeast mixture and olive oil alternately, stirring with a wooden spoon after each addition. Turn out the dough onto a lightly floured work surface and knead for 8 minutes until the dough is soft and elastic. Place the dough in a large, lightly oiled bowl and leave to rise until doubled in size, about 1 hour.

Punch down the dough and divide into six balls. Put each ball, one by one, onto a floured surface, then flatten and shape into a circle with a rolling pin. Cover each circle with plastic wrap (clingfilm) and leave to rest for 5 more minutes. Run the rolling pin over the circles again until they are about 8" (20cm) in diameter. Use the rounds immediately, or layer them between pieces of baking parchment, cover, and refrigerate for up to 4 hours.

Preheat the grill to high on one side, warm on the other. Brush one side of the base with oil. Place the base oiled-side down on the hot side of the grill. Cook until grill marks appear, 2–3 minutes. Turn the dough over and add toppings. When the bottom has browned, slide the pizza to the cooler side of the grill. Close the lid and cook until the toppings are hot and the cheese has melted.

These can be made using any of the pesto recipes on pages 178–181. Just follow exactly the same method substituting your favorite pesto.

Pesto flatbreads

FINGER FOOD | Makes 1 flatbread

- 1 x 12" (30cm) Crispy pizza base (see page 36)
- 3 Tbsp pesto of choice (see pages 178–181)
- 3–4 basil leaves, torn
- 1 oz. (25g) pine nuts, toasted
- Extra virgin olive oil, for brushing

Roll the pizza base so it is ready to be topped. Preheat the oven to 425°F/220°C/gas mark 7.

Spread the pesto over half of the round, leaving a ½" (1cm) border uncovered around the edge. Sprinkle with the torn basil and pine nuts. Fold the uncovered side of the round over the filling and press the edges together to seal them. Using a sharp knife, make diagonal cuts through the top at ¾" (2cm) intervals, exposing the pesto mixture. Brush the dough with olive oil. Place on a lightly floured baking sheet and cook in the middle of the preheated oven for 10–12 minutes or until crispy and golden and the base sounds hollow when tapped.

Using a large knife or pizza cutter, cut the flatbread into strips using the diagonal cuts as a guide and serve immediately or at room temperature.

Of course, you could just use store-bought tortillas to make your pizzas, but there is nothing more satisfying than making your own. The slightly irregular shapes that you may end up with also add to the enjoyment.

Quick tortilla pizza base

CRISPY, QUICK | Makes 8 x 10"–12" (25–30cm) pizzas

- 10½ oz. (300g) plain flour
- ½ tsp fine salt
- 6½ fl. oz. (190ml) water
- 3 Tbsp olive oil

Combine the flour and salt in a large bowl. Stir in the water and oil until combined. Transfer to a lightly floured surface and knead about 10–12 times, adding extra flour or water if needed to form a smooth dough. Cover the dough and leave to rest for about 10 minutes.

Divide the dough into eight equal portions approximately 2–2½ oz. (60–70g) each. On a lightly floured surface, roll each portion into a 10"–12" (25–30cm) circle. Stack the rolled tortillas between lightly floured baking parchment until you are ready to cook them.

Heat a large, nonstick frying pan coated with oil spray. Cook the tortillas, one at a time, for approximately 1 minute on each side or until lightly golden. Allow to cool before topping as a pizza.

Cooked topped tortillas in an oven preheated to 400°F/200°C/gas mark 6 for approximately 8–10 minutes or until golden and crispy. Serve immediately.

Our take on a gluten-free crust is thin, chewy, and serves many today, tomorrow, or the next day. Yes, this dough lives happily covered loosely in the fridge for up to five days. Just take a handful when you need a quick pizza. Easy gluten-free living at its best.

Gluten-free base

CRISPY, SIMPLE | Makes 4–5 x 12" (30cm) thin-crust pizza rounds

- 1 lb. (450g) gluten-free blended flour (we use Bob's Red Mill)
- 4 ½ oz. (130g) cornmeal
- 1 Tbsp dried granular yeast
- 1 tsp salt
- 1 Tbsp cornstarch (corn flour)
- 13 ½ fl. oz. (400ml) lukewarm water
- 2 ½ fl. oz. (60ml) olive oil
- 1 egg
- 1 Tbsp honey (or maple syrup, agave syrup, date syrup, or sugar)

In a large mixing bowl or the bowl of a stand mixer fitted with a dough hook, combine flour, cornmeal, yeast, salt, and cornstarch. In a separate bowl, whisk together water, olive oil, egg, and honey, then add to the dry ingredients and stir until dough pulls together into a smooth mixture. Get your hands in there (turn motor off if using a mixer!) to get all the flour from the bottom of the bowl incorporated into the dough. Add more gluten-free flour, a few spoonfuls at a time, if the mixture is sticky.

Cover bowl with a tea towel and leave dough to rise for about 2 hours, at room temperature. It won't grow large like traditional wheat-based doughs, but it will become spongy to the touch.

Place dough in the fridge until needed. When ready to bake, preheat oven to 400°F/200°C/gas mark 6. Take an 8 oz. (225g) portion of dough from the fridge, roughly form into a ball, and place on a piece of baking parchment dusted with gluten-free flour. Cover dough with another dusting of flour and another layer of baking parchment, then roll dough between the parchment until it's about ⅛" (5mm) thick. Peel off the top parchment and slide dough, with parchment still beneath, onto a baking tray or pizza stone. Top with desired toppings and bake for 10–12 minutes or until toppings are cooked to your liking and base has cooked through.

Any remaining dough can be kept in the refrigerator for up to five days.

These are a great way to start a casual dinner party. Just make sure your guests don't fill up on pizza breads.

Pizza breads

SAVORY | Makes 4 breads

❭ 1 quantity Crispy pizza base dough (see page 36)

TOPPING SUGGESTIONS

❭ Leaves from 2 rosemary stalks, finely chopped + 1 tsp sea salt + 1 clove garlic, crushed + 2 Tbsp extra virgin olive oil

❭ 2 Tbsp extra virgin olive oil + 2 Tbsp capers, rinsed, drained, and roughly chopped +

1 clove garlic, crushed + ground black pepper

❭ 1 Tbsp chili oil + 1 tsp thyme leaves + 1 oz. (30g) Gruyère cheese, finely grated

❭ Sea salt + freshly ground black pepper + 1 Tbsp extra virgin

olive oil + 3 ½ oz. (100g) mozzarella, cubed

❭ 1 Tbsp extra virgin olive oil + 4 anchovy fillets + 1 clove garlic, all crushed together

❭ 2 Tbsp pesto (see pages 178–181) + 2 ¾ oz. (75g) mozzarella

Make the Crispy pizza base dough up to the point where you have four individual dough balls. Shape each ball into 10"–12" (25–30cm) rounds, prick evenly four to five times with a fork, transfer to a baking sheet, and rest for 10 minutes.

Preheat the oven to 425°F/220°C/gas mark 7. For all toppings suggestions, combine all the ingredients, except the cheese (if using), and brush over the whole pizza base using a pastry brush. Then sprinkle on the cheese, if using. Cook in the middle of the oven for 8–10 minutes or until golden and crispy. Cut into wedges and serve immediately.

This is a substantial but not-too-heavy pizza base.

Focaccia pizza base

AIRY | Makes 2 x 10" (25cm) pizzas

> 2 tsp dried granular yeast
> 9 fl. oz. (250ml) lukewarm water
> 1 lb. 2 oz. (500g) plain flour
> 1 tsp salt
> 3 Tbsp olive oil

Sprinkle the yeast into the water. Leave to dissolve for 5–10 minutes. Combine the flour (reserving about 2 Tbsp for kneading) and salt in a large bowl and make a well in the center. Pour in the olive oil and yeasted water. Using a wooden spoon, work the ingredients together by pulling the flour into the liquid mixture until it comes together, adding a little additional water if necessary. Using your hands, transfer the mixture to a lightly floured surface. Knead the dough for 10 minutes or until it is smooth, silky, and elastic in texture. Form the dough into a ball and put in a clean, lightly oiled bowl. Cover with a clean tea towel and leave to rise for about 1–1½ hours or until doubled in size.

Once doubled in size, knock the dough back and knead for 5 more minutes. Cut the dough into two even-sized pieces, press out flat, and, using a floured rolling pin, shape into about 10" (25cm) rounds. Cover again and leave to rest for 15–20 more minutes.

Preheat the oven to 425°F/220°C/gas mark 7. Using the tips of your fingers, make shallow indentations all over the surface of the dough. The dough is now ready to be topped. Cook on a lightly floured baking sheet in the middle of the oven for 14–16 minutes or until golden and the base is cooked through.

Sweet dough requires a little more kneading than savory dough in order to get to the same silky, smooth texture.

Sweet honey pizza base

SUBTLE | Makes 2 x 12" (30cm) thick-crust bases
or 4 x 12" (30cm) thin-crust bases

- 2 tsp dried granular yeast
- 4 fl. oz. (125ml) lukewarm water
- 6 fl. oz. (175ml) lukewarm whole milk
- 6 fl. oz. (175ml) clear (runny) honey
- 1 Tbsp extra virgin olive oil
- 1 large egg, beaten
- Finely grated zest of 1 lemon
- ¼ oz. (8g) saffron powder (optional)
- 1 tsp salt
- 1 lb. 4 oz.–1 lb. 5 oz. (550–600g) plain flour

Sprinkle the yeast into the water. Leave to dissolve for 5–10 minutes. Add the milk, honey, oil, egg, lemon zest, and saffron (if using) to the yeast mixture and stir well. Sift the salt and flour into the wet mixture and mix to a dough, adding additional flour if necessary to form a ball. Transfer the mixture to a lightly floured surface and knead for 10–15 minutes or until smooth and elastic. Return the dough to a clean bowl and leave covered for about 1½ hours or until doubled in size.

Knock the dough back and divide into two or four, depending on the desired thickness of the base required, and shape into 10"–12" (25–30cm) rounds. Leave the dough to rest for 10–15 minutes.

Preheat the oven to 425°F/220°C/gas mark 7. Add your toppings. Cook the pizzas in the middle of the oven for 10–12 minutes for a thin base or 15–18 minutes for a thicker base or until lightly golden and crispy.

The simple cauliflower pizza base is a perfect innovative, plant-inspired pizza crust. This is our version of this new classic, which features coconut flour and a pinch of ground coriander. We like to top it with Cilantro (coriander) pesto (page 180), a good sprinkling of crumbled feta, and lots of soft greens. It's a salad, it's a pizza, it's a celebration of flavor.

Cauliflower pizza base

HEALTHY, UNIQUE | Makes 1 pizza

› 1 head cauliflower, chopped (approximately 1 lb. 9 oz./720g of florets)
› 2 eggs
› 3½ oz. (100g) coconut flour
› 1 tsp ground coriander seed
› ½ tsp sea salt
› Ground black pepper
› Olive oil (to grease pan)

Preheat oven to 400°F/200°C/gas mark 6.

Line baking tray with baking parchment and grease with olive oil.

Blend cauliflower florets in batches in a food processor, until florets become tiny bits—some call this the "cauliflower rice" stage, and I think it resembles cooked couscous. Transfer to a big bowl and whisk in eggs. Add coconut flour, ground coriander, sea salt, and pepper. Mix together using your hands, then scoop mixture onto parchment-lined and greased baking tray. With the help of a spatula, form into a large rectangle about ½" (1cm) thick.

Bake for 20 minutes or until edges are golden and center is firm. Remove from the oven and top with toppings of choice, then return to the oven, if desired, to cook toppings. Possible toppings include tomato sauce, pesto, soft cheeses like fresh mozzarella, blanched or fresh greens, seeds, asparagus, grilled vegetables like zucchini (courgettes) or peppers, and more.

Classics

In Naples there is only one pizza. It begins with the simple recipe of water, yeast, flour, and salt. The water activates the yeast, the flour feeds it, and the moist, warm air allows it all to grow. Experienced hands stretch it into a circle. Simple toppings such as tomatoes, fresh basil, and mozzarella are scattered on top. A long wooden paddle inserts it into a domed wood-fired oven. Temperatures inside the oven range from 675°F (357°C) on the floor to 950°F (510°C) on the ceiling. Such temperatures will cook a pizza in 80 to 120 seconds. The crust is puffy and charred, thin yet chewy. It's simple yet specific. To a Neapolitan, it's the only way.

Pizza wasn't invented in Naples, or Italy for that matter. Nevertheless, the Neapolitan pizza, with its charred, puffed-up crust and light, tomato-based toppings, is undoubtedly the best in the world. Out of respect for this simple fact, we bring you a chapter devoted entirely to the classic pizzas of Naples and its surrounding areas.

This was the original, first-ever Neapolitan pizza—simplicity at its best!

Marinara

NEAT | Makes 1 pizza

- 1 x 12" (30cm) Crispy pizza base (see page 36)
- 7 oz. (200g) cherry tomatoes, halved
- ⅛ tsp salt
- 2 Tbsp extra virgin olive oil
- 1 clove garlic, thinly sliced
- 1 tsp dried oregano
- Sea salt and freshly ground black pepper

Prepare the pizza base so it is ready to be topped. Preheat the oven to 425°F/220°C/gas mark 7.

Halve the tomatoes and place in a sieve over a bowl. Press the tomatoes firmly with the back of a spoon to release as much liquid as possible. Sprinkle on the ⅛ tsp salt and leave to drain for 10 more minutes. Brush the base with half of the olive oil. Scatter the tomatoes over the pizza base, leaving a ½"–¾" (1–2cm) border uncovered around the edge. Scatter on the garlic slices and oregano.

Cook in the middle of the preheated oven for 10–12 minutes or until crispy and golden. Remove from the oven, drizzle with a little more olive oil, season with sea salt and freshly ground black pepper, and serve.

This simple pizza is a great accompaniment to soup or salads. Pizza at its best!

Margherita

UNADULTERATED | Makes 1 pizza

> 1 x 12" (30cm) Crispy pizza base (see page 36)
> 4 fl. oz. (125ml) Quick classic tomato sauce (see page 186)
> 2¾ oz. (75g) mozzarella, cubed
> 5–6 basil leaves, torn
> Sea salt
> 1 Tbsp extra virgin olive oil

Prepare the pizza base so it is ready to be topped. Preheat the oven to 425°F/220°C/gas mark 7. Spread the tomato sauce evenly over the base, leaving a ½"–¾" (1–2cm) border uncovered around the edge. Scatter on the mozzarella and torn basil leaves. Sprinkle on some salt and drizzle over the olive oil. Cook in the center of the preheated oven for 10–12 minutes or until crispy and golden. Serve immediately.

This one is for Stuart West, our friend and photographer who helps make our books so enjoyable to do. He likes it spicy!

Piccante

SPICY | Makes 1 pizza

- 1 x 12" (30cm) Crispy pizza base (see page 36)
- 4 fl. oz. (125ml) Spicy tomato sauce (see page 184)
- 3½ oz. (100g) pepperoni slices
- 8–12 black olives, pitted
- 2 oz. (50g) grated Parmesan cheese
- Chili oil, to serve (optional)

Preheat the oven to 425°F/220°C/gas mark 7. Prepare the pizza base so it is ready to be topped.

Evenly spread the tomato sauce over the base, leaving a ½"–¾" (1–2cm) border uncovered around the edge. Place the pepperoni slices on top, scatter on the olives, and sprinkle on the Parmesan. Cook in the middle of the preheated oven for 10–12 minutes or until crispy and golden. Drizzle with chili oil when it comes out of the oven, if desired, and serve immediately.

This pizza is covered with seafood. It takes a little longer to prepare, and probably a little longer to eat—but it's worth it!

Frutti di mare

COLORFUL | Makes 1 pizza

- 1 x 12″ (30cm) Crispy pizza base (see page 36)
- 4 fl. oz. (125ml) Spicy tomato sauce (see page 184)
- 3½ oz. (100g) small mussels, in their shells and well rinsed
- 3½ oz. (100g) clams, in their shells and well rinsed
- 6-8 whole raw shrimp (prawns)
- 1 clove garlic, finely chopped
- 1 handful flat-leaf parsley, chopped
- Sea salt and freshly ground black pepper
- Extra virgin olive oil

Preheat the oven to 425°F/220°C/gas mark 7. Prepare the pizza base so it is ready to be topped.

Bring a large pan of slightly salted water to boil. Run the mussels and clams under cold running water and discard any that do not close when tapped sharply. Remove any beards and barnacles from the mussels. Quickly boil the mussels and clams in the water, for 1–2 minutes or until steamed open, then drain well. Discard any that do not open. Set aside to cool slightly.

Spread the tomato sauce evenly over the base, leaving a ½″–¾″ (1–2cm) border uncovered around the edge. Scatter on the well-drained mussels and clams evenly and then add the shrimp (prawns). Scatter on the garlic and half of the parsley and season well. Drizzle with oil and cook in the middle of the preheated oven for 10–12 minutes or until crispy and golden around the edges. Serve immediately, sprinkled with the remaining parsley.

If you are serving this pizza to egg lovers, then you may want to add extra eggs and position them so that when cut into pieces, each person gets a yolk. Just be careful, when you are cracking them onto the base, that they don't ooze everywhere!

Florentina

OOZING | Makes 1 pizza

- 1 x 12" (30cm) Crispy pizza base (see page 36)
- 4 fl. oz. (125ml) Quick classic tomato sauce (see page 186)
- 1 clove garlic, thinly sliced
- 6 oz. (180g) baby spinach leaves, blanched and well drained
- 3½ oz. (100g) mozzarella, sliced
- Grated fresh nutmeg
- 1 oz. (20g) finely grated Parmesan cheese
- 1 green (spring) onion, finely sliced
- 2 eggs
- Extra virgin olive oil
- Freshly ground black pepper

Preheat the oven to 425°F/220°C/gas mark 7. Prepare the pizza base so it is ready to be topped.

Evenly spread the tomato sauce over the base, leaving a ½"–¾" (1–2cm) border uncovered around the edge. Scatter the garlic, spinach, and mozzarella over the sauce. Finely grate a little nutmeg all over the pizza and sprinkle on the Parmesan and green (spring) onion. Cook in the middle of the preheated oven for 6 minutes, then open the oven, pull out the rack, and quickly crack the eggs onto the center of the pizza. Return to the oven and cook for 4–6 more minutes or until crispy and golden. Once cooked, drizzle with oil and a grind of black pepper, then serve immediately.

Quattro stagioni means "four seasons," and this pizza should be made with the toppings placed in four sections, representing each season. However, if you are sharing the pizza, it makes more sense to distribute the ingredients around more evenly so everybody gets a little bit of everything.

Quattro stagioni

HEARTY | Makes 1 pizza

› 1 x 12" (30cm) Crispy pizza base (see page 36)
› 2½ fl. oz. (75ml) Quick classic tomato sauce (see page 186)
› 4 slices Parma ham
› 2 tomatoes, thinly sliced
› 2 oz. (50g) small mushrooms, thinly sliced
› 1 Tbsp capers, rinsed and drained
› 8–12 black olives, pitted
› 4–6 anchovy fillets
› 5 oz. (150g) mozzarella, sliced
› Extra virgin olive oil

Prepare the pizza base so it is ready to be topped. Preheat the oven to 425°F/220°C/gas mark 7.

Spread the tomato sauce evenly over the pizza base, leaving about ½"–¾" (1–2cm) uncovered around the edge. Tear the Parma ham into strips and place over the sauce. Evenly scatter all the remaining ingredients (except the mozzarella and oil) over the ham, then top with the sliced mozzarella.

Cook in the middle of the preheated oven for 10–12 minutes or until crisp and golden. Remove from the oven, drizzle with a little extra virgin olive oil, and serve immediately.

One of life's simple pleasures: bread served with cheese. Accompany this pizza with a good Chianti and we assure you you'll be happy!

Quattro formaggi

RICH | Makes 1 pizza

- 1 x 12" (30cm) Crispy pizza base (see page 36)
- 2¾ oz. (75g) ricotta
- 2 oz. (50g) mozzarella, sliced
- 2 oz. (50g) Gorgonzola, sliced
- 1¼ oz. (30g) Parmesan cheese, finely grated
- Freshly ground black pepper

Prepare the pizza base so it is ready to be topped. Preheat the oven to 425°F/220°C/gas mark 7.

Put spoonfuls of ricotta here and there all over the pizza, leaving a ½"–¾" (1–2cm) border uncovered around the edge. Scatter on the mozzarella and Gorgonzola slices, then sprinkle on the Parmesan. Cook in the middle of the preheated oven for 10–12 minutes or until crispy and golden. Remove from the oven, season with black pepper, and serve immediately.

Tip: Sprinkle on a handful of basil leaves or arugula (rocket) for a bit of color just before serving.

This is a classic pizza in which mushrooms are truly given the chance to shine. Speaking of mushrooms, don't feel obliged to stick to the ordinary variety. If your tomatoes lack luster, follow the Tip below.

Funghi

EARTHY | Makes 1 pizza

- 1 x 12" (30cm) Crispy pizza base (see page 36)
- 4-5 mixed ripe tomatoes (about 1 lb. 2 oz./500g), blanched, peeled, deseeded, and chopped (see Tip at right)
- ⅛-¼ tsp salt
- 4 oz. (120g) chestnut mushrooms, finely chopped
- 10-15 fresh oregano leaves, roughly chopped
- 5 oz. (150g) mozzarella, sliced
- Extra virgin olive oil, for drizzling
- Salt and freshly ground black pepper

Prepare the pizza base so it is ready to be topped. Preheat the oven to 425°F/220°C/gas mark 7.

Place the prepared tomatoes in a sieve and sprinkle with ⅛-¼ tsp salt. Allow to drain for 10 minutes, pushing firmly with the back of a spoon to release excess liquid. Spoon the tomatoes over the pizza base, leaving about ½"-¾" (1-2cm) uncovered around the edge. Top with mushrooms, oregano, and slices of mozzarella. Finish with a drizzle of olive oil and salt and pepper to taste.

Cook in the middle of the preheated oven for 10-12 minutes until the crust is golden and the cheese is bubbling. Serve immediately.

Tip: If ripe tomatoes aren't available, use any of the tomato recipes featured in the Sauces chapter (see pages 178-187).

This classic concoction is the Italian version of the meat-lovers' pizza. To maintain classic status, be sure to use ripe tomatoes, fresh mozzarella, and the best charcuterie available.

Capricciosa

MACHO | Makes 1 pizza

> 1 x 12" (30cm) Crispy pizza base (see page 36)
> 12 oz. (350g) mixed ripe tomatoes
> ⅛ tsp salt
> 1 clove garlic, crushed
> 1 small white onion, thinly sliced
> 3½ oz. (100g) chestnut mushrooms, thinly sliced
> 2 oz. (50g) pepperoni slices
> 2 oz. (50g) salami slices
> 2 oz. (50g) prosciutto slices
> 2 oz. (50g) black olives
> 5 oz. (150g) mozzarella, sliced
> Sea salt and freshly ground black pepper

Prepare the pizza base so it is ready to be topped. Preheat the oven to 425°F/220°C/gas mark 7.

Roughly chop the tomatoes and place in a sieve over a bowl. Press the tomatoes firmly with the back of a spoon to release as much liquid as possible. Sprinkle with salt (and a pinch of sugar if the tomatoes aren't very sweet) and leave to drain for 10 more minutes.

Spoon the tomatoes over the base, leaving about ½"–¾" (1–2cm) uncovered around the edge, and sprinkle with crushed garlic. Top with the remaining ingredients and season with sea salt and pepper to taste. Bake for 10–12 minutes or until the cheese has melted and the crust is golden. Serve immediately.

This is a classic Italian pizza and sauce. The dark, briny, hot nature of the traditional ingredients—capers, anchovies, black olives, and chilies—make for a very fine pizza.

Puttanesca

EXTRA ZING | Makes 1 pizza

- 1 x 12″ (30cm) Crispy pizza base (see page 36)
- ½ quantity Sweet cherry tomato sauce (see page 183)
- 8 anchovy fillets in oil, drained
- 10 kalamata olives
- 2 Tbsp capers
- 1 tsp finely chopped peperoncini (see Tip at right)
- 3 Tbsp grated Parmesan cheese
- Extra virgin olive oil, for drizzling
- 2 Tbsp roughly chopped flat-leaf parsley

Prepare the pizza base so it is ready to be topped. Preheat the oven to 425°F/220°C/gas mark 7.

Spoon the Sweet cherry tomato sauce over the pizza base, leaving about ½″–¾″ (1–2cm) uncovered around the edge. Top with anchovies, olives, capers, peperoncini, and Parmesan. Cook in the middle of the preheated oven for 10–12 minutes until crust is golden and cheese is bubbling. Remove from the oven and finish with a drizzle of olive oil and a sprinkling of parsley. Serve immediately.

Tip: Peperoncini are small, red, slightly sweet Italian chilies. If not available, use any type of red chili.

A pure, (almost) perfectly white pizza, which the Italians aptly name Bianca. Such simple, clean flavors deserve the best ingredients. Reach for flaky sea salt, firm garlic, and the freshest mozzarella you can find to do it full justice.

Bianca

CLEAN | Makes 1 pizza

⟩ 1 head garlic
⟩ 1 x 12" (30cm) Crispy pizza base (see page 36)
⟩ 2 Tbsp olive oil
⟩ 5 oz. (150g) mozzarella, sliced
⟩ 1 tsp sea salt
⟩ 1 sprig fresh rosemary, needles removed and chopped

Preheat the oven to 425°F/220°C/gas mark 7.

Wrap the whole head of garlic in foil and roast for 45 minutes until soft. Cool slightly. Slice the top off the garlic head and squeeze the cloves into a bowl. Stir with a fork.

Prepare the pizza base so it is ready to be topped.

Brush the pizza base with 1 Tbsp olive oil. Distribute slices of mozzarella over the base, leaving about ½"–¾" (1–2cm) uncovered around the edge, then top with sea salt, garlic, and chopped rosemary. Drizzle with the remaining olive oil.

Bake for 10–12 minutes or until the cheese has melted and the crust is golden. Serve immediately.

Land and sea

Combining meat and seafood recipes in one chapter is a bold move. There are meat lovers, there are vegetarians, and there are vegetarians who dabble in seafood. Some meat lovers enjoy seafood. Some don't. Some vegetarians fish, but don't eat their catch. Others are firmly against the consumption of seafood of any kind. And here you have land and sea pizzas, seemingly thrown together in one careless chapter.

But there's a catch. The land and sea do not join. You will not find surf and turf pizzas on the following pages, where meat and seafood are featured together on one confused pizza. No, we firmly believe land and sea are separate entities to be enjoyed exclusively on their own. Never the twain shall meet. Well, rarely.

Pizza is a perfect vehicle for fruits from the sea. The soft, chewy base is a seafood vessel. Pizza is also the perfect vehicle for meat. The elusive saltiness penetrates tomatoes, mingles with cheese, and is punctuated by sea salt.

Land and sea. Enjoy them, one at a time.

This is a speciality from Nice in southern France. It is actually an open tart, but it can be made with bread dough or pastry. We make it with pizza dough, so, in our minds, it becomes a pizza!

Pissaladière

CLASSIC | Makes 1 pizza

- 1 x 12" (30cm) Thick-crust pizza base (see page 38)
- 2 quantities Caramelized onions (see page 187)
- 2¾ oz. (75g) anchovy fillets, halved lengthways
- About 20 black olives, pitted
- 1 tsp fresh thyme leaves
- Extra virgin olive oil, to serve

Preheat the oven to 425°F/220°C/gas mark 7. Roll the pizza base into a rectangular shape, about 12" (30cm) long and 8" (20cm) wide, and leave to rest for about 10 minutes.

Evenly spread the Caramelized onions over the base, leaving a ½"–¾" (1–2cm) border uncovered around the edge. Arrange the anchovy fillets in a checkerboard pattern with rows about 1½" (4cm) apart and on the diagonal. Place an olive in the center of each diamond and sprinkle on the thyme leaves. Cook in the middle of the preheated oven for 14–16 minutes or until crispy and golden and the base is cooked through. Remove from the oven, drizzle with extra virgin olive oil, and serve hot or cold.

This pizza works really well on the grill. Just cook the base, then add the
toppings for a perfect summer meal or snack with a green salad on the side.

Tomato salsa, salmon, and caper

FRESH | Makes 1 pizza

- 1 x 12″ (30cm) Crispy pizza base (see page 36)
- 2 Tbsp extra virgin olive oil
- 2 Tbsp capers, rinsed, drained, and roughly chopped
- 1 clove garlic, crushed
- ½ red onion, finely chopped
- 2 tomatoes, deseeded and finely chopped
- Juice of ½ lemon
- 1 Tbsp chopped fresh dill
- Sea salt and freshly ground black pepper
- 4 oz. (125g) smoked salmon slices
- Crème fraîche, to serve (optional)

Prepare the pizza base so it is ready to be topped. Preheat the oven to 425°F/220°C/gas mark 7.

Combine the olive oil, capers, and garlic in a small bowl and brush over the whole pizza base. Cook in the middle of the preheated oven for 8–10 minutes or until crispy and golden.

While the base is cooking, prepare the salsa. Combine the red onion, chopped tomatoes, lemon juice, and dill in a small bowl and season well. When the base is cooked, remove it from the oven and lay the smoked salmon slices evenly over it, leaving a ½″–¾″ (1–2cm) border uncovered around the edge. Scatter on the tomato salsa and serve immediately. Serve with a dollop of crème fraîche on each piece if desired.

These are great after a big night out and are best served hot.

All-day breakfast calzone

WHOLESOME | Makes 6 calzoni

> 1 quantity Calzone dough (see page 38)
> 30–36 Slow-roasted tomatoes (see page 182) or sun-dried tomatoes
> 9–12 sausages (about 1 lb. 5 oz./600g)
> 10 oz. (300g) mozzarella, sliced
> 6 slices Parma ham
> 6 medium eggs
> Salt and freshly ground black pepper
> Extra virgin olive oil

Preheat the oven to 425°F/220°C/gas mark 7.

Divide the dough into six pieces. Put a piece of baking parchment on a work surface and roll out one ball of dough into a 8" (20cm) round. Reserve the remaining balls in a bowl covered with a clean tea towel. Evenly place 5–6 tomatoes over half of the round, leaving a ½" (1cm) border uncovered around the edge. Squeeze the sausage meat from about two casings into teaspoon-sized balls. Top with 2 oz. (50g) sliced mozzarella and one torn-up piece of Parma ham. Make a small crater-like hollow in the middle of the assembled ingredients. Crack 1 egg into the crater, reserving a little of the egg white, and season with salt and pepper. Working quickly, fold the uncovered side of the round over the filling and press the edges together to seal them and form a crescent shape. Brush with egg white. Carefully transfer to a baking sheet and bake for 15 minutes or until the crust is golden and the bottom of the calzone is cooked through. Allow to rest for a few minutes before serving.

While the calzone is cooking, continue preparing the remaining calzoni. You can make and cook more than one calzone at a time.

We would always make this pizza using a thin, crispy base so that it somewhat resembles the pancake that you would normally wrap your Peking duck in.

Duck, hoisin, and green (spring) onion

ASIAN | Makes 1 pizza

- 1 x 12" (30cm) Crispy pizza base (see page 36)
- 2 Tbsp hoisin sauce
- 2 Peking duck legs, cooked and meat shredded
- 2 green (spring) onions, finely shredded
- Extra virgin olive oil or chili oil

Prepare the pizza base so it is ready to be topped. Preheat the oven to 425°F/220°C/gas mark 7.

Spread the hoisin sauce evenly over the pizza base, leaving a ½" (1cm) border uncovered around the edge. Evenly scatter the duck and green (spring) onions over the sauce and drizzle all over with a little oil. Cook in the middle of the preheated oven for 10–12 minutes or until crispy and golden. Serve immediately.

Lindsay's cousins used to own a business, St. Mary's River Smokehouses, that produced the best hot-smoked salmon we've ever tasted. It was smoked using maple syrup, which imparts a succulent, sweet flavor. Fingers crossed you can find something similar . . .

Walnut pesto and hot-smoked salmon

INDULGENT | Makes 1 pizza

- 1 x 12" (30cm) Crispy pizza base (see page 36)
- 2 Tbsp Walnut pesto (see page 180)
- 2 Tbsp crème fraîche
- 5 oz. (150g) hot-smoked salmon
- 1 small chicory, finely shredded (optional)
- 3½ oz. (100g) mozzarella, sliced
- Salt and freshly ground black pepper
- 2 oz. (50g) watercress
- Extra virgin olive oil

Prepare the pizza base so it is ready to be topped. Preheat the oven to 425°F/220°C/gas mark 7.

Combine the Walnut pesto and crème fraîche and spread evenly over the base, leaving about a ¾" (2cm) border uncovered around the edge. Scatter on the hot-smoked salmon, chicory (if using), and mozzarella. Season generously with salt and freshly ground black pepper. Cook in the middle of the preheated oven for 10–12 minutes or until golden and crispy. Remove from the oven, sprinkle on the watercress, drizzle with extra virgin olive oil, and serve immediately.

The base for this pizza is topped with Slow-roasted tomato sauce (see page 183). The slow-roasting really intensifies the flavor of the tomatoes. Leave the little tails on the shrimp (prawns) for an authentic look.

Shrimp (prawn) and arugula (rocket)

FRAGRANT | Makes 1 pizza

- 1 x 12" (30cm) Crispy pizza base (see page 36)
- ½ quantity Slow-roasted tomato sauce (see page 183)
- 8–12 peeled raw shrimp (prawns), tails left on
- 5 oz. (150g) mozzarella, sliced
- Sea salt and freshly ground black pepper
- 2 oz. (50g) arugula (rocket) leaves
- Extra virgin olive oil or chili oil

Prepare the pizza base so it is ready to be topped. Preheat the oven to 425°F/220°C/gas mark 7.

Spread the Slow-roasted tomato sauce evenly over the pizza base, leaving about a ¾" (2cm) border uncovered around the edge. Evenly place the shrimp (prawns) and sliced mozzarella over the sauce. Season with salt and pepper.

Cook in the middle of the preheated oven for 10–12 minutes or until crispy and golden. Remove from the oven, sprinkle on the arugula (rocket) leaves, drizzle with oil, and serve immediately.

Pizza with canned tuna—you either love it or you hate it! With the Spicy tomato sauce (see page 184) and salty capers, though, it really is a good pizza topping.

Pizza al tonno

STORE-CUPBOARD | Makes 1 pizza

- 1 x 12" (30cm) Crispy pizza base (see page 36)
- 4 fl. oz. (125ml) Spicy tomato sauce (see page 184)
- 5½ oz. (160g) canned tuna in oil, drained
- 2 Tbsp capers
- 3 sprigs fresh thyme, leaves removed
- 3½ oz. (100g) mozzarella, sliced
- Extra virgin olive oil, for drizzling
- Basil leaves, torn, to serve

Prepare the pizza base so it is ready to be topped. Preheat the oven to 425°F/220°C/gas mark 7.

Spread the tomato sauce over the pizza base, leaving about a ¾" (2cm) border uncovered around the edge. Evenly spread the tuna over the tomato sauce. Sprinkle on the capers and thyme leaves and top with the mozzarella slices. Finally, drizzle with a little extra virgin olive oil.

Cook in the middle of the preheated oven for 10–12 minutes or until crispy and golden. Remove from the oven, drizzle with a little more extra virgin olive oil, and top with freshly torn basil leaves. Serve immediately.

Sausage meat on a pizza isn't always as crass as the offerings of your local pizza delivery company. Choose top-quality sausages and you will realize how good it can be!

Spicy tomato, sausage, and fennel seed

FRAGRANT | Makes 1 pizza

- 1 x 12" (30cm) Crispy pizza base (see page 36)
- 4 fl. oz. (125ml) Spicy tomato sauce (see page 184)
- 7 oz. (200g) pork sausage meat (about 3 sausages)
- 1 red pepper, roasted, peeled, and sliced
- 1 tsp fennel seeds
- 3½ oz. (100g) mozzarella, sliced
- Extra virgin olive oil, for drizzling
- 1 small handful basil leaves, torn

Prepare the pizza base so it is ready to be topped. Preheat the oven to 425°F/220°C/gas mark 7.

Spread the tomato sauce over the pizza base, leaving about ½"–¾" (1–2cm) uncovered around the edge. Evenly spread the sausage meat, in mounds of about 1 tsp, over the sauce. Top with the roasted pepper slices, fennel seeds, and mozzarella slices. Drizzle with a little olive oil.

Cook in the middle of the preheated oven for 10–12 minutes or until crispy and golden. Remove from the oven, drizzle with a little more extra virgin olive oil, and top with freshly torn basil leaves. Serve immediately.

It's the sauce that really makes this pizza special. Try serving it with Basil pesto (see page 178).

Red pepper sauce, chicken, and olive

SIMPLE | Makes 1 pizza

> 1 large skinless chicken breast
> 1 x 12" (30cm) Crispy pizza base (see page 36)
> 4 fl. oz. (125ml) Tomato and roasted red pepper sauce (see page 184)
> 3½ oz. (100g) mascarpone
> Finely grated rind of 1 lemon
> Freshly ground black pepper
> 1 tsp fresh thyme leaves
> 12 green olives
> Extra virgin olive oil
> Basil pesto (optional) (see page 178)

Poach the chicken breast in a small pan of simmering water for 12–15 minutes or until cooked. Remove from the water and set aside to cool, then slice into about 10–12 thin slices.

Prepare the pizza base so it is ready to be topped. Preheat the oven to 425°F/220°C/gas mark 7.

Spread the Tomato and roasted red pepper sauce over the pizza base, leaving about a ½"–¾" (1–2cm) border uncovered around the edge. Evenly place the chicken slices over the sauce. Combine the mascarpone, lemon rind, pepper, and thyme in a small bowl, then place spoonfuls of this mixture evenly over the base. Top with the green olives and drizzle with a little extra virgin olive oil.

Cook in the middle of the preheated oven for 10–12 minutes or until crispy and golden. Remove from the oven, drizzle with the pesto (if using) or a little more olive oil, and serve immediately.

We love using ricotta on pizzas because the nature of it means that it doesn't melt when cooked.

Spinach, pancetta, and ricotta

RUSTIC | Makes 1 pizza

- 1 x 12" (30cm) Crispy pizza base (see page 36)
- 5 oz. (150g) cubed pancetta
- 4 oz. (125g) ricotta cheese
- 1 pinch nutmeg
- 3 green (spring) onions, finely sliced
- 1 egg
- Freshly ground black pepper
- 2½ fl. oz. (60ml) Quick classic tomato sauce (see page 186)
- 7 oz. (200g) fresh spinach, washed, blanched, and well drained
- Extra virgin olive oil

Prepare the pizza base so it is ready to be topped. Preheat the oven to 425°F/220°C/gas mark 7.

Heat a small nonstick frying pan and add the pancetta cubes. Cook for 3–4 minutes or until golden and crispy. Set aside on a paper towel (kitchen paper). Mix the ricotta cheese, nutmeg, half of the green (spring) onions, egg, and black pepper in a small bowl until just combined (do not beat the mixture). Spread the tomato sauce over the pizza base, leaving about a ½"–¾" (1–2cm) border uncovered around the edge. Spoon the ricotta mixture evenly over the tomato. Top with the spinach leaves, pancetta, and remaining green (spring) onion slices.

Cook in the middle of the preheated oven for 10–12 minutes or until crispy and golden. Remove from the oven, drizzle with a little extra virgin olive oil, and serve immediately.

Since this isn't such an authentic combination of pizza toppings, we like to make it on our Thick-crust pizza base (see page 38). It becomes more like a large toasted sandwich and is good eaten hot or cold.

Chicken, cranberry, and brie

SWEET | Makes 1 pizza

- 2 small chicken breasts
- 1 x 12″ (30cm) Thick-crust pizza base (see page 38)
- 4 Tbsp store-bought cranberry sauce
- 3½ oz. (100g) brie, sliced
- 4 Tbsp Caramelized onions (see page 187)
- Freshly ground black pepper
- Extra virgin olive oil

Put the chicken breasts in a pan of simmering water and poach for 10–12 minutes or until cooked through. Remove from the water and set aside to cool slightly (this can be done up to a day in advance).

Prepare the pizza base so it is ready to be topped. Preheat the oven to 425°F/220°C/gas mark 7.

Spread the cranberry sauce evenly over the pizza base, leaving about a ½″–¾″ (1–2cm) border uncovered around the edge. Slice the chicken breasts and spread evenly over the sauce. Top with the brie slices, Caramelized onions, and a good grind of black pepper.

Cook in the middle of the preheated oven for 14–16 minutes or until crispy and golden and the base is cooked. Remove from the oven, drizzle with a little extra virgin olive oil, and serve immediately.

Try this with Parma ham instead of bresaola if you prefer—it works well too!

Fennel relish and beef carpaccio

TEXTURAL | Makes 1 pizza

> 1 x 12" (30cm) Crispy pizza base (see page 36)
> 1 quantity Caramelized fennel relish (see page 185)
> 5 oz. (150g) mozzarella, cubed
> 2¾ oz. (75g) bresaola slices (about 8–10 slices)
> Handful flat leaf parsley, roughly chopped
> Extra virgin olive oil, to serve

Prepare the pizza base so it is ready to be topped. Preheat the oven to 425°F/220°C/gas mark 7.

Evenly spread the fennel relish over the base, leaving a ½"–¾" (1–2cm) border uncovered around the edge. Scatter on the mozzarella and cook in the middle of the preheated oven for 10–12 minutes or until crispy and golden. Remove from the oven and place the bresaola on the pizza, allowing about 1 piece per slice. Scatter on the parsley and drizzle with a little oil. Serve immediately.

If you can't get hold of Thai basil, which should be available from specialty supermarkets, then just use regular basil. It still imparts a slightly aniseedy flavor and is also delicious with the chili and chicken.

Sweet chili, shredded chicken, and basil

AROMATIC | Makes 1 pizza

> ⟩ 1 x 12" (30cm) Crispy pizza base (see page 36)
> ⟩ 2–3 Tbsp store-bought sweet chili sauce
> ⟩ 1 small leek, halved lengthways and finely sliced
> ⟩ 5–6 Thai basil leaves, torn
> ⟩ 2 cooked chicken breasts, shredded
> ⟩ Extra virgin olive oil or chili oil

Prepare the pizza base so it is ready to be topped. Preheat the oven to 425°F/220°C/gas mark 7.

Spread the sweet chili sauce evenly over the base, leaving about a ½"–¾" (1–2cm) border uncovered around the edge. Scatter on the sliced leek and basil leaves, then the chicken. Drizzle all over with extra virgin olive oil or chili oil.

Cook in the middle of the preheated oven for 10–12 minutes or until crispy and golden. Remove from the oven and drizzle with a little more oil. Serve immediately.

This pizza is based on one of my favorite salads. The salad comes from Julie Le Clerc's Simple Café Food, and, with the addition of chorizo and spinach, I think it makes a perfect pizza topping.

Tomato, pumpkin, chorizo, and spinach

BOLD | Makes 1 pizza

- 1 lb. 2 oz. (500g) pumpkin, peeled and cut into about ¾" (2cm) cubes
- Extra virgin olive oil
- 1 x 12" (30cm) Crispy pizza base (see page 36)
- 3–4 Tbsp (about ½ quantity) Sun-dried tomato pesto (see page 181)
- 6 oz. (180g) spinach, blanched and well drained
- 3½ oz. (100g) uncooked chorizo, cut into small cubes
- 5 oz. (150g) mozzarella, sliced
- Sea salt and freshly ground black pepper

Preheat the oven to 425°F/220°C/gas mark 7.

Put the cubed pumpkin in a roasting dish and drizzle on 1 tsp olive oil. Toss to coat. Roast the pumpkin for 15–20 minutes or until cooked and golden. Set aside to cool slightly. Prepare the pizza base so it is ready to be topped.

Spread the Sun-dried tomato pesto evenly over the pizza base, leaving about a ½"–¾" (1–2cm) border uncovered around the edge. Evenly spread the spinach, chorizo, and pumpkin over the sauce. Top with the sliced mozzarella and season well. Cook in the middle of the preheated oven for 10–12 minutes or until crispy and golden. Remove from the oven, drizzle with a little extra virgin olive oil, and serve immediately.

This rustic Italian pizza is a real autumn treat when wild mushrooms are in abundance.

Wild mushroom, radicchio, and bresaola

AUTUMNAL | Makes 1 pizza

- 1 x 12″ (30cm) Crispy pizza base (see page 36)
- 1 Tbsp extra virgin olive oil
- 1 clove garlic, crushed
- 9 oz. (250g) mixed wild mushrooms of choice
- 1 small radicchio, roughly shredded
- Freshly ground black pepper
- 5 oz. (150g) soft goat's cheese
- 3–4 zucchini (courgette) flowers (optional)
- 2¾ oz. (75g) bresaola slices
- 1 small bunch flat-leaf parsley, roughly chopped
- Chili oil, to serve

Prepare the pizza base so it is ready to be topped. Preheat the oven to 425°F/220°C/gas mark 7.

Heat the olive oil in a frying pan over high heat. When the pan is very hot, add the garlic, mushrooms, and radicchio and sauté for 1–2 minutes or until the mushrooms are just wilted but not releasing liquid. Season generously with black pepper and set aside.

Spread the goat's cheese over the base, leaving a ½″–¾″ (1–2cm) border uncovered around the edge. Scatter on the mushrooms and radicchio and top with zucchini (courgette) flowers if using. Cook in the middle of the preheated oven for 10–12 minutes or until crispy and golden. Remove from the oven, top with the bresaola and parsley, and drizzle with chili oil. Serve immediately.

Make sure you wait for a few minutes before digging into these delicious calzoni—they'll be piping hot inside!

Calabrese, mushroom, and cheese calzone

HEARTY | Makes 6 calzoni

- 1 quantity Calzone dough (see page 38)
- 1 quantity Quick classic tomato sauce (page 186)
- 3½ fl. oz. (100ml) Black olive tapénade (see page 185) (optional)
- 6 oz. (175g) (24 thin slices) calabrese salami
- 6½ oz. (180g) feta cheese, crumbled
- 6½ oz. (180g) chèvre
- 10 oz. (300g) block mozzarella, grated
- 14 oz. (400g) chestnut mushrooms, thinly sliced
- 3 ripe tomatoes, each cut into 8 wedges

Preheat the oven to 425°F/220°C/gas mark 7. Divide the pizza dough into six pieces. Put a piece of baking parchment on a work surface and roll out one ball of dough into a 8" (20cm) round. Reserve the remaining balls in a bowl covered with a clean tea towel.

Spoon 2 Tbsp tomato sauce and 1 Tbsp of the tapénade (if using) over the base. On one half of the round place 3-4 slices calabrese, 1 oz. (30g) feta, 1 oz. (30g) chèvre, 2 oz. (50g) mozzarella, a handful of mushroom slices, and 4 tomato wedges. Fold the other half of the round over the filling and pinch the edges together to form a crescent shape.

Carefully transfer the baking parchment to a baking sheet and bake for 15 minutes or until crust is golden and the bottom of the calzone is cooked through. Allow to rest for a few minutes before serving. While the calzone is cooking, continue preparing the remaining calzoni. You can make and cook more than one calzone at a time.

Cilantro (coriander) pesto, packed with mint, garlic, chili, and walnuts, adds an incredible depth of flavor to tender shrimp (prawns) and salty feta cheese.

Cilantro (coriander) pesto, shrimp (prawn), and feta

FRESH | Makes 1 pizza

- 1 x 12" (30cm) Crispy pizza base (see page 36)
- 2 heaped Tbsp Cilantro (coriander) pesto (see page 180)
- 8–12 raw shrimp (prawns), peeled (see Tip at right)
- 2¾ oz. (75g) feta cheese, crumbled

Prepare the pizza base so it is ready to be topped. Preheat the oven to 425°F/220°C/gas mark 7. Prepare the pesto and set aside.

Spoon the pesto over the pizza base, leaving a ½"–¾" (1–2cm) border uncovered around the edge. Top with shrimp (prawns), turning to coat in pesto. Finish with crumbled feta. Bake for 10–12 minutes until the crust is golden. Serve immediately.

Tip: Cooked, frozen shrimp (prawns) can be substituted for fresh. Follow the recipe as above, except sauté the shrimp (prawns) to defrost and to remove excess moisture.

A sweet, smoky, hearty pizza that is always a crowd pleaser.

Barbecued chicken

SUBSTANTIAL | Makes 1 pizza

- 1 x 12" (30cm) Crispy pizza base (see page 36)
- 1 quantity Caramelized onions (see page 187)
- 10 oz. (300g) skinless chicken breasts
- 1 Tbsp olive oil
- 3½ fl. oz. (100ml) + 2 Tbsp Mustard bourbon barbecue sauce (see page 187 and Tip at right)
- 7 oz. (200g) Monterey Jack cheese, grated
- 2 Tbsp chopped cilantro leaves (coriander)

Prepare the pizza base so it is ready to be topped. Preheat the oven to 425°F/220°C/gas mark 7.

Prepare the Caramelized onions and set aside. Cut the chicken breasts into bite-sized pieces. Heat the olive oil in a large frying pan over medium-high heat. Add the chicken and sauté until cooked through, about 6 minutes. Allow to cool slightly. In a large bowl, toss the chicken with 2 Tbsp of the barbecue sauce, cover, and refrigerate.

Spread 3½ fl. oz. (100ml) of the barbecue sauce over the base, leaving a ½"–¾" (1–2cm) border uncovered around the edge. Top with Caramelized onions and chicken pieces, and finish with grated cheese. Bake for 10–12 minutes until the crust is golden and the cheese is bubbling. Sprinkle with cilantro (coriander) and serve immediately.

Tip: Our Mustard bourbon barbecue sauce (see page 187) is delicious, but, if you are short on time, your favorite store-bought barbecue sauce will make a fine alternative.

Pancetta lends a wonderful salty-smoky quality to this unique pizza.

Asiago, pancetta, and chicory

SOPHISTICATED | Makes 1 pizza

- 1 x 12″ (30cm) Crispy pizza base (see page 36)
- 1 Tbsp olive oil
- 5 oz. (150g) pancetta, cubed
- 5 heads chicory, chopped crossways and ends discarded
- 3 Tbsp freshly grated Parmesan cheese
- Juice of ½ lemon
- Sea salt and ground black pepper to taste
- 5 oz. (150g) Asiago cheese, grated

Prepare the pizza base so it is ready to be topped. Preheat the oven to 425°F/220°C/gas mark 7.

Heat the olive oil in a large frying pan over medium-high heat. Add the pancetta and sauté until the edges begin to brown. Add the chicory and sauté, stirring occasionally, until it begins to wilt, about 5 minutes. Remove from the heat and stir in the Parmesan and lemon juice. Season with salt and pepper and set aside.

Spoon the chicory mixture over the base, leaving a ½″–¾″ (1–2cm) border uncovered around the edge, and cover with cheese. Bake for 10–12 minutes until the crust is golden and cooked through in the center. Remove from the oven, cool slightly, and serve.

Peaches and prosciutto are a wonderful combination, making sweet harmony on a pizza.

Caramelized onion, prosciutto, and peach

SUMMERY | Makes 1 pizza

- 1 quantity Caramelized onions (see page 187)
- 1 x 12" (30cm) Crispy pizza base (see page 36)
- 8 pieces thinly sliced prosciutto, torn
- 2 small peaches, each cut into 8 wedges
- 2¾ oz. (75g) chèvre, crumbled
- Freshly ground black pepper to taste

Prepare the Caramelized onions and set aside. Prepare the pizza base so it is ready to be topped. Preheat the oven to 425°F/220°C/gas mark 7.

Spoon the onions over the base, leaving a ½"–¾" (1–2cm) border uncovered around the edge. Top with pieces of prosciutto and 12 peach wedges (eat the extras!). Finish with crumbled chèvre and ground pepper.

Bake for 10–12 minutes until the crust is golden. Serve immediately.

Here, simple flavors come together to create something far greater than the sum of their parts.

Basil pesto, Genoa salami, and mozzarella

SAVORY | Makes 1 pizza

- 1 x 12" (30cm) Crispy pizza base (see page 36)
- 2 heaped Tbsp Basil pesto (see page 178)
- 5 oz. (150g) mozzarella, sliced
- 3 oz. (80g) Genoa salami, thinly sliced
- Freshly ground black pepper
- Basil leaves, to serve

Prepare the pizza base so it is ready to be topped. Preheat the oven to 425°F/220°C/gas mark 7.

Spread the pesto over the base, leaving a ½"–¾" (1–2cm) border uncovered around the edge. Cover with mozzarella and top with salami. Finish with a twist of black pepper.

Bake for 10–12 minutes or until the cheese has melted and the crust is golden. Serve immediately, topped with basil leaves.

This colorful, spring-like pizza is best made with a thick crust. The asparagus and cherry tomatoes sink into the dough like a soft, chewy pillow.

Asparagus, bacon, and cherry tomato

COLORFUL | Makes 1 pizza

- 1 x 12″ (30cm) Thick-crust pizza base (see page 38)
- 5 slices bacon, chopped into ¾″ (2cm) pieces, or 2 oz. (50g) pancetta, cubed
- 7 oz. (200g) mozzarella, sliced
- 5 oz. (150g) fresh asparagus, woody stems removed, chopped
- 7 oz. (200g) cherry tomatoes, halved
- 2 oz. (50g) goat's cheese, crumbled
- Freshly ground black pepper
- Chili oil

Prepare the pizza base so it is ready to be topped. Preheat the oven to 425°F/220°C/gas mark 7.

Put the cubes of bacon in a large frying pan and set over medium-high heat. Cook until the fat is released and the bacon is just browned. Remove the bacon with a slotted spoon and drain on a paper towel (kitchen paper).

Place mozzarella slices over the base, leaving a ½″–¾″ (1–2cm) border uncovered around the edge. Top with bacon slices, chopped asparagus, and cherry tomatoes. Finish with crumbled goat's cheese and pepper to taste. Bake for 12–14 minutes until the crust is golden and the base is cooked through in the center. Remove from the oven, drizzle with chili oil, and serve immediately.

From the garden

Pippa and I are fine gardeners. We water our potted window herbs with care and attention. We lovingly snip leaves from pristine store-bought basil plants. These are qualities one needs when creating garden-inspired pizzas. Each season brings bountiful produce. With the winter comes purple-sprouting broccoli and king cabbages. The spring welcomes asparagus, wild fennel, and new potatoes. Baby greens, zucchini (courgettes), and corn mark the summer. Autumn is defined by pumpkins, wild mushrooms, and Jerusalem artichokes.

All right—Pippa and I are actually urban gardeners. We carry baskets rather than spades. It's not our fault; there's concrete where soil should be. But our parents are good gardeners, and we paid attention. We understand seasonality and respect locally grown produce. We coddle our fruits and vegetables. We water with care. And most of all, we're excellent weeders. One has to be when there are countless recipes that could have made their way into this delicious chapter. Once the results came in, we had to weed, and weed again. Gardening, after all, is hard work.

This white pizza is also delicious made on a Focaccia pizza base (see page 52).
Try a drizzle of chili oil just before serving if heat is your thing.

Jerusalem artichoke pizza bianca

SOPHISTICATED | Makes 1 pizza

- 1 x 12" (30cm) Crispy pizza base (see page 36)
- 2 Tbsp extra virgin olive oil
- 2 Tbsp capers, roughly chopped
- 1 clove garlic, crushed
- 10 oz. (300g) Jerusalem artichokes, parboiled for 5 minutes then sliced lengthways about ¼" (5mm) thick
- 3½ oz. (100g) mozzarella, sliced
- Freshly ground black pepper
- 1–2 bunches cherry tomatoes on the vine

Prepare the pizza base so it is ready to be topped. Preheat the oven to 425°F/220°C/gas mark 7.

Combine the olive oil, capers, and garlic in a small bowl. Brush the oil mixture all over the base using a pastry brush. Place the artichoke slices evenly over the base, leaving a ½"–¾" (1–2cm) border uncovered around the edge. Add the mozzarella and a good grind of black pepper. Place the cherry tomatoes on top.

Cook in the middle of the preheated oven for 10–12 minutes or until crisp and golden. Serve immediately.

This pizza is quite rich, so we like to serve it with a large green salad on the side.

Mushroom, rosemary, and ricotta

RUSTIC | Makes 1 pizza

- 1 x 12″ (30cm) Crispy pizza base (see page 36)
- 1 oz. (30g) dried porcini mushrooms, soaked in warm water
- Extra virgin olive oil
- 1 onion, finely chopped
- 1 tsp finely chopped rosemary
- 1 clove garlic, crushed
- 4 oz. (125g) ricotta
- 7 oz. (200g) chestnut mushrooms, sliced
- 3½ oz. (100g) mozzarella, sliced
- 2 oz. (50g) arugula (rocket) leaves

Prepare the pizza base so it is ready to be topped. Preheat the oven to 425°F/220°C/gas mark 7.

Drain the porcini mushrooms, squeezing out any excess water, and chop finely. Heat 1 Tbsp extra virgin olive oil in a nonstick frying pan and add the onion. Cook for 2–3 minutes or until translucent but not browned. Add the rosemary, garlic, and chopped porcini and sauté for 2–3 more minutes. Remove from the heat and cool slightly. Stir in the ricotta and spread the mixture evenly over the base, leaving a ½″–¾″ (1–2cm) border uncovered around the edge. Evenly scatter on the chestnut mushrooms and slices of mozzarella.

Cook in the middle of the preheated oven for about 10–12 minutes or until crisp and golden. Remove from the oven. Sprinkle on the arugula (rocket), drizzle with extra virgin olive oil, and serve immediately.

This is a great pizza in which to use up any leftover roasted vegetables.

Roasted vegetable and taleggio

NOURISHING | Makes 1 pizza

- 2 zucchini (courgettes), halved lengthways and cut into chunks
- 1 red or yellow pepper, cut into ⅝" (1.5cm) cubes
- 1 red onion, peeled and cut into wedges
- 1 sprig rosemary, needles removed
- 1 tsp extra virgin olive oil
- 1 x 12" (30cm) Crispy pizza base (see page 36)
- 4 fl. oz. (125ml) Quick classic tomato sauce (see page 186)
- 3½ oz. (100g) taleggio cheese, sliced
- Salt and freshly ground black pepper
- 2 Tbsp Parsley pesto (see page 179), to serve (optional)

Prepare the roasted vegetables (this can be done up to 2 days in advance). Preheat the oven to 400°F/200°C/gas mark 6. Put the zucchini (courgettes), pepper, onion, and rosemary in a roasting dish. Drizzle on the olive oil and toss to coat. Roast the vegetables for about 15–20 minutes or until cooked and golden. Set aside to cool slightly.

Prepare the pizza base so it is ready to be topped. Preheat the oven to 425°F/220°C/gas mark 7.

Spread the tomato sauce over the base, leaving about a ½"–¾" (1–2cm) border uncovered around the edge. Evenly spread the vegetables over the sauce and top with the taleggio. Season well.

Cook in the middle of the preheated oven for 10–12 minutes or until crispy and golden. Remove from the oven, drizzle with the pesto (if using), and serve immediately.

I used to think that potato and bread eaten together was far too heavy—until I had this dish at Books for Cooks in London.

Arugula (rocket) and new potato focaccia

NOURISHING | Makes 1 pizza

⟩ ½ quantity Focaccia pizza base dough (see page 52)

⟩ 4 Tbsp Arugula (rocket) pesto (see page 179)

⟩ 10 oz. (300g) new potatoes, parboiled for 8–10 minutes then sliced lengthways, about ¼" (5mm) thick

⟩ 1½ oz. (40g) grated Gruyère cheese

⟩ Sea salt and freshly ground black pepper

⟩ 2 oz. (50g) arugula (rocket) leaves

⟩ Chili oil, to serve

On a lightly floured work surface, roll out the dough into a rectangular shape about 12" (30cm) long and 8" (20cm) wide. Place on baking parchment or a baking sheet ready to be topped and leave to rest for 15–20 minutes. Preheat the oven to 425°F/220°C/gas mark 7.

Make small indentations on the top of the dough using your fingertips. Spread the Arugula (rocket) pesto evenly over the base, leaving about a ½"–¾" (1–2cm) border around the edges. Evenly place the potatoes over the pesto so they slightly overlap. Sprinkle on the Gruyère and season with salt and pepper. Cook in the middle of the preheated oven for about 14–16 minutes or until crisp and golden and the base is cooked through. Remove from the oven, then throw on some fresh arugula (rocket) leaves and a drizzle of chili oil to serve.

London's Portobello Road market on a Saturday morning is a great place to pick up a quick and tasty snack. It's where I was inspired to create this pizza.

Roasted red onion, artichoke, and sage

SIMPLICITY | Makes 2 long pizzas

- 2 red onions, peeled and cut into thin wedges
- 7 oz. (200g) marinated artichokes, drained and quartered
- 12–16 sage leaves
- 1 tsp extra virgin olive oil
- ¼ quantity Crispy pizza base dough (see page 36)
- 3½ fl. oz. (100ml) Quick classic tomato sauce (see page 186)
- 1¼ oz. (30g) finely grated Parmesan cheese
- Chili oil, to serve

Preheat the oven to 425°F/220°C/gas mark 7. Put the onion, artichokes, and sage leaves in a roasting tray with 1 tsp extra virgin olive oil. Cook for 15–20 minutes or until golden and starting to go crispy.

Divide the pizza dough into two balls. On a lightly floured surface, roll each ball into an oblong shape about 10" (25cm) long and 4" (10cm) wide. Transfer the bases to a baking sheet ready to be topped and leave to rest.

Spread the tomato sauce evenly over the bases, leaving about a ½" (1cm) border around the edge. Evenly scatter on the red onion wedges, artichoke quarters, sage leaves, and Parmesan. Cook in the middle of the preheated oven for 10–12 minutes or until golden and crispy. Serve immediately with chili oil drizzled over.

Slightly charred broccoli is a delicious addition to any pizza. Kale and the leaves of brussels sprouts also pair well with the saltiness of the halloumi, so choose whatever greens you have available.

Broccoli, halloumi, and sauerkraut

HEALTHY, NOURISHING | Makes 1 pizza

- 1 x 12" (30cm) Ancient spelt and quinoa pizza base (see page 40)
- 2–2¾ oz. (50-75g) soft goat's cheese
- 2¼ oz. (60g) sauerkraut
- 1 tsp caraway seeds
- 6-8 stems tenderstem broccoli, lightly blanched
- 2 oz. (50g) halloumi, coarsely grated
- 2 oz. (50g) mozzarella, grated

Prepare the pizza base so it is ready to be topped. Preheat the oven to 425°F/220°C/gas mark 7.

Spread, or crumble, the goat's cheese evenly over the pizza base, leaving a ½" (1cm) border. Top with the sauerkraut, caraway seeds, broccoli, halloumi, and mozzarella.

Cook in the middle of the preheated oven for 10–12 minutes or until golden and crispy. Remove from the oven and serve immediately.

If you're like us and think weekend breakfasts should include something buttery and flaky, something salty, and the perfect egg, it's time to embrace the breakfast pizza. It's a pizza with a tart-like twist that's equal parts delicious, sophisticated, and easy! It will easily feed 2–4 people.

Breakfast pizza

LIVELY, BRIGHT | Makes 1 pizza

- 8 oz. (225g) frozen puff pastry, thawed
- 5 eggs
- 4 fl. oz. (125ml) crème fraîche
- 2½ oz. (70g) feta cheese, crumbled
- Zest of 1 lemon
- ½ tsp herbes de Provence
- ⅛ tsp sea salt
- 6 asparagus spears, trimmed
- 4 slices prosciutto, sliced in half
- Microgreens, to garnish (optional)
- Sea salt and cracked black pepper

Preheat oven to 400°F/200°C/gas mark 6.

Unroll thawed puff pastry onto a baking tray. Cut a ½" (1cm) strip off each side of the pastry and set aside. Crack one egg into a small bowl and whisk well. Prick pastry all over with a fork and brush with whisked egg. Lay strips of pastry onto the edge of the pastry to create a raised "crust," then brush edges with egg as well. Bake pastry until golden, about 10–12 minutes. Center will puff a little; ease it back down with your hand as it is cooling.

Meanwhile, combine crème fraîche, feta cheese, lemon zest, herbes de Provence, and sea salt in a small bowl. Stir well to combine. Spread mixture within the framed edges of the pastry. Top with asparagus spears (any design will do) and torn pieces of prosciutto, leaving a small well in four areas for each egg to nestle in. Now crack eggs, one at a time, into a little bowl. Scoop egg up with your fingers to drain off not the whites, but the excess "water" that sometimes surrounds the whites. Place the eggs in the wells of the pizza.

Bake for 15 minutes or until egg whites have cooked through and yolks are still a little soft. Slice and top with microgreens before serving.

Tip: Equal parts sour cream or ricotta can be substituted for crème fraîche in this recipe.

We love the combination of mint and zucchini (courgettes). For a non-vegetarian version, tear a few slices of Parma ham and scatter on just before serving.

Grilled zucchini (courgette), mint, and goat's cheese

SPRINGTIME | Makes 1 pizza

- 1 x 12" (30cm) Crispy pizza base (see page 36)
- 2 medium zucchini (courgettes), sliced lengthways about ⅛"–¼" (3–4 mm) thick (see Tip at right)
- 1 Tbsp extra virgin olive oil
- 1 clove garlic, crushed
- 6–8 mint leaves, finely sliced, plus extra to serve
- Sea salt and freshly ground black pepper
- ½ quantity Sweet cherry tomato sauce (see page 183)
- 3½ oz. (100g) goat's cheese

Prepare the pizza base so it is ready to be topped. Preheat the oven to 425°F/220°C/gas mark 7.

Heat a grill pan to very hot and grill the zucchini (courgette) slices for 2–3 minutes on the first side and 1–2 minutes on the second side or until cooked through. Remove from the heat and combine with the oil, garlic, and sliced mint leaves. Season well and set aside.

Evenly spread the tomato sauce over the base, leaving a ½"–¾" (1–2cm) border around the edge. Scatter on the zucchini (courgette) slices and crumble on the goat's cheese. Cook in the middle of the preheated oven for 10–12 minutes or until crispy and golden. Remove from the oven and scatter on a few extra mint leaves. Serve immediately.

Tip: Use a combination of green and yellow zucchini (courgettes), if they are available, for an impressive look.

Our Sweet cherry tomato sauce is made using a little honey, which goes particularly well with the Gorgonzola.

Cherry tomato, leek, and Gorgonzola

SUBSTANTIAL | Makes 1 pizza

> 1 x 10" (25cm) Focaccia pizza base (see page 52)

> ½ quantity Sweet cherry tomato sauce (see page 183)

> 1 medium leek, trimmed, halved, and finely sliced (about 3¼ oz./90g)

> 3½ oz. (100g) Gorgonzola cheese, cubed

> Freshly ground black pepper

> Extra virgin olive oil

> 4-6 basil leaves

Prepare the pizza base so it is ready to be topped. Preheat the oven to 425°F/220°C/gas mark 7.

Spread the Sweet cherry tomato sauce evenly over the base, leaving a ½"–¾" (1–2cm) border around the edge. Evenly spread the sliced leek and Gorgonzola over the sauce and grind on some black pepper. Finally, drizzle with a little extra virgin olive oil.

Cook in the middle of the preheated oven for 14–16 minutes or until crispy and golden and the base is cooked through. Remove from the oven and drizzle with a little more extra virgin olive oil. Scatter on the basil leaves and serve immediately.

The cheese oozes out when these calzoni are cut, so it is best to let them rest for a few minutes before tucking in.

Red pepper and eggplant (aubergine) calzone

HEARTY | Makes 6 calzoni

- Extra virgin olive oil
- 3 medium eggplants (aubergines), cut into ½" (1cm) cubes
- Salt and freshly ground black pepper
- 1 quantity Calzone dough (see page 38)
- 10 fl. oz. (300ml) Tomato and roasted red pepper sauce (see page 184)
- 10 oz. (300g) mozzarella, sliced
- 5 oz. (150g) grated Parmesan cheese
- 1 handful basil leaves, torn

Heat 2–3 tsp olive oil in a large nonstick frying pan and sauté the eggplant (aubergine) cubes until golden and cooked. Season to taste and set aside to cool slightly. Preheat the oven to 425°F/220°C/gas mark 7.

Divide the dough into six pieces. Put a piece of baking parchment on a work surface and roll out one ball of dough into a 8" (20cm) round. Reserve the remaining dough balls in a bowl covered with a clean tea towel.

Spread about 3–4 Tbsp of the sauce over one half of the base, leaving ¾" (2cm) as a rim. Evenly spread on one-sixth of the eggplants (aubergines) and top with 2 oz. (50g) mozzarella, 1 oz. (25g) Parmesan, and a few basil leaves. Fold the uncovered half of the dough over the filling and, using your fingers, crimp the edge to seal it, forming a crescent shape.

Transfer the parchment to a baking sheet and bake for 15 minutes or until the crust is golden and the bottom of the calzone is cooked. Rest for a few minutes before serving. While the calzone is cooking, prepare the remaining calzoni. You can make and cook more than one calzone at the same time.

This pizza is full of flavor and packed with goodness.

Salsa verde and artichoke

GREEN | Makes 1 pizza

- 1 x 12" (30cm) Crispy pizza base (see page 36)
- 3–4 anchovy fillets
- 2 Tbsp capers, rinsed
- 1 small bunch flat-leaf parsley (about ⅛ oz./5g)
- 1 clove garlic
- 5 oz. (150g) artichoke hearts, drained and quartered
- 3½ oz. (100g) mozzarella, sliced
- 2 oz. (50g) arugula (rocket) leaves
- Freshly ground black pepper
- Extra virgin olive oil

Prepare the pizza base so it is ready to be topped. Preheat the oven to 425°F/220°C/gas mark 7.

To make the salsa verde, use a large, sharp knife and roughly chop the anchovy fillets, capers, parsley, and garlic. Combine to form a coarse paste. Spread the salsa verde over the base, leaving a ½"–¾" (1–2cm) border around the edge, and top with the artichoke quarters. Top with the mozzarella slices.

Cook in the middle of the preheated oven for 10–12 minutes or until golden and crispy. Remove from the oven and top with the arugula (rocket) leaves and a good grind of fresh black pepper. Drizzle on a little extra virgin olive oil and serve immediately.

This unique combination creates a gently sweet, tart, yet pungent pizza. The light, simple toppings make a perfect accompaniment to a soup or salad.

Pear, Gouda, and cumin

INTRIGUING | Makes 1 pizza

- 1 x 12" (30cm) Crispy pizza base (see page 36)
- 9 oz. (250g) Gouda cheese, grated
- 1 large Bosc pear (see Tip at right)
- ½ tsp cumin seeds
- 1 Tbsp pine nuts, toasted
- Extra virgin olive oil, for drizzling
- Sea salt to taste
- Basil leaves, to serve

Prepare the pizza base so it is ready to be topped. Preheat the oven to 425°F/220°C/gas mark 7.

Sprinkle the Gouda evenly over the base, leaving a ½"–¾" (1–2cm) border around the edge. Slice the pear into thin slices from top to bottom around the core. Discard the core. Distribute the pear slices over the cheese and sprinkle with cumin seeds and pine nuts. Drizzle with olive oil and a sprinkling of sea salt. Bake until the cheese has melted and the crust is golden. Serve immediately, topped with torn basil leaves.

Tip: Bosc pears are large, slender pears with rust-colored skin that hold their shape well when baked. Any pear, however, will do. Increase the quantity if the pears are small.

A pizza stone, which creates a very hot, professional environment in the oven, is useful for this pizza. The lush, colorful ingredients are piled so high that extra heat is helpful.

Tomato, sweet potato, and red onion

CARAMELIZED | Makes 1 pizza

- 2 large red onions
- 2 Tbsp olive oil
- 1 tsp extra-fine (caster) sugar
- Salt and pepper
- 12 oz. (350g) mixed ripe tomatoes
- 1 x 12" (30cm) Crispy pizza base (see page 36)
- 1 small sweet potato, peeled and thinly sliced
- 1 sprig fresh rosemary, needles removed and chopped
- 9 oz. (250g) taleggio cheese, cut into ½" (1cm) cubes

Preheat the oven to 425°F/220°C/gas mark 7.

Peel the onions and cut each onion into 8 wedges. Place them in an oven roasting pan, toss with olive oil and sugar, and season with salt and pepper to taste. Roast the onions in the oven for 30 minutes, stirring every 10 minutes, until slightly charred and caramelized. Remove from the heat.

Roughly chop the tomatoes and place in a sieve over a bowl. Press the tomatoes with the back of a spoon to release as much liquid as possible. Sprinkle with ⅛ tsp salt (and a pinch of sugar if the tomatoes aren't very sweet) and leave to drain for 10 minutes.

Prepare the pizza base so it is ready to be topped. Spoon the tomatoes evenly onto the base, leaving a ½"–¾" (1–2cm) border around the edge. Top with red onions, sweet potato, rosemary, and cheese. Bake for 12–15 minutes until the crust is golden and the center is cooked through. Cool slightly, then slice and serve with forks and knives—toppings need taming with this pizza!

Colors and flavors abound in this hot, sour, and salty-sweet pizza.

Mango salsa, pesto, and goat's cheese

FUSION | Makes 1 pizza

- 1 x 12″ (30cm) Crispy pizza base (see page 36)
- 2 heaped Tbsp Cilantro (coriander) pesto (see page 180)
- 3½ oz. (100g) goat's cheese, crumbled

FOR THE MANGO SALSA

- 1 mango, peeled, pitted, and the flesh finely cubed
- 1 small red pepper, cored and finely cubed
- 4 oz. (120g) red onion, finely chopped
- ¾ oz. (20g) fresh cilantro leaves (coriander), finely chopped
- 1 red chili, deseeded and finely chopped
- 2 fl. oz. (50ml) sweet chili sauce
- Juice of 1 lime

Prepare the pizza base so it is ready to be topped. Preheat the oven to 425°F/220°C/gas mark 7.

Spread the base with Cilantro (coriander) pesto. Place the salsa ingredients in a small bowl and stir to combine. Spoon half of the salsa over the base, leaving a ½″–¾″ (1–2cm) border around the edge, and reserve the rest for use in another recipe. (It is excellent with tortilla or pita chips and will keep in the fridge for 24 hours). Top with the crumbled goat's cheese.

Bake for 10–12 minutes until the crust is golden and cooked through in the center. Serve immediately.

This simple, juicy pizza is filled with layers of intriguing flavors and textures.

Tomato, chicory, and blue cheese

DISTINCTIVE | Makes 1 pizza

- 1 x 12″ (30cm) Crispy pizza base (see page 36)
- ½ quantity Sweet cherry tomato sauce (see page 183)
- 1 Tbsp olive oil
- 4 heads chicory, finely sliced, ends discarded
- 2 oz. (50g) radicchio, finely sliced
- Sea salt and ground black pepper
- 5 oz. (150g) cambozola or any creamy blue cheese, roughly sliced

Prepare the pizza base so it is ready to be topped. Preheat the oven to 425°F/220°C/gas mark 7. Prepare the Sweet cherry tomato sauce and set aside.

Heat the olive oil in a heavy-bottomed frying pan over medium-high heat. Add the sliced chicory and radicchio and sauté, stirring occasionally, until wilted and slightly translucent, about 5 minutes. Season with sea salt and ground black pepper. Spoon the cherry tomato sauce onto the base, leaving a ½″–¾″ (1–2cm) border around the edge. Add the sautéed chicory and radicchio and finish with slices of cambozola.

Bake in the middle of the oven for 10–12 minutes or until the crust is golden. Remove from the oven and allow to rest for 1–2 minutes. Slice and serve immediately.

This woodsy, flavorful pizza, filled with vitamin-rich spinach and the essential vitamins and minerals of mushrooms, will simultaneously satiate and enrich the body. That's a lot for one little pizza.

Wild mushroom, havarti, and spinach

SEASONAL | Makes 1 pizza

- 1 x 12" (30cm) Crispy pizza base (see page 36)
- 1 Tbsp olive oil
- 2 cloves garlic, finely chopped
- 7 oz. (200g) mixed wild mushrooms
- 5 oz. (150g) fresh spinach, trimmed and washed
- ¼ tsp sea salt
- ⅛ tsp freshly ground black pepper
- 2 Tbsp Basil pesto (see page 178)
- 4-5 sage leaves, finely chopped
- 9 oz. (250g) havarti cheese, cut into ½" (1cm) cubes

Prepare the pizza base so it is ready to be topped. Preheat the oven to 425°F/220°C/gas mark 7.

Heat the olive oil in a frying pan and add the garlic and mushrooms. Sauté for 2–3 minutes, stirring regularly, until the garlic is fragrant and the mushrooms are coated. Add the spinach and stir, occasionally, until wilted. Sprinkle with sea salt and pepper and remove the pan from the heat.

Spread the pesto evenly over the base, leaving a ½"–¾" (1–2cm) border around the edge. Top with the mushroom and spinach mixture, sage leaves, and cubed havarti. Bake for 12–15 minutes until the cheese and crust are golden. Serve immediately.

Rainbow chard is a beautiful spring green with stalks ranging in color from pale green to gold to bright red. Its cousin, Swiss chard, makes a perfectly suitable alternative.

Rainbow chard, garlic, and feta

ELECTRIC | Makes 1 pizza

> 1 x 12″ (30cm) Crispy pizza base (see page 36) or 1 Thick-crust pizza base (see page 38)
> 1 bunch (about 1 lb. 2 oz./500g) rainbow chard, ribs discarded
> 2 Tbsp olive oil
> 2 cloves garlic, crushed
> Sea salt and ground black pepper
> 7 oz. (200g) block mozzarella, grated
> 3½ oz. (100g) feta cheese, crumbled
> 1 Tbsp chili oil

Prepare the pizza base so it is ready to be topped. Preheat the oven to 425°F/220°C/gas mark 7.

Bring a large pan of salted water to boil. Add the chard and cook just until tender, about 2 minutes. Drain, rinse with cold water, drain again, and squeeze out excess water. Transfer the chard to a chopping board and roughly chop. Heat the olive oil in a large frying pan and add the garlic. Sauté until fragrant, about 30 seconds, then add the chopped chard. Sauté for 1 more minute, then season with salt and pepper to taste.

Cover the base with mozzarella, leaving a ½″–¾″ (1–2cm) border around the edge, then add the cooked chard. Top with feta and drizzle with chili oil. Bake for 10–12 minutes for the thin base, 12–14 minutes for the thick base, until the crust is golden and cooked through in the center. Serve immediately.

Grilling pizza is pure bliss, as long as you follow three basic rules. 1: Use our Grilled pizza base dough recipe. It's soft, yet dense enough to keep its shape on the grill. 2: Accept that this will be a casual, eat-when-it's-ready meal. 3: The topping we've given is just a suggestion. Experiment with whatever ingredients you have on hand. This pizza can only be cooked on a grill with a lid.

Grilled pizza with red onion and pesto

TOOTHSOME | Makes 6 pizzas

>) 1 quantity Cilantro (coriander) pesto (see page 180)
>) 6 x 8" (20cm) Grilled pizza bases (see page 45)
>) Extra virgin olive oil, for brushing
>) 1 red onion, thinly sliced
>) 5 oz. (150g) goat's cheese, sliced

Prepare the pesto and set aside.

Preheat the grill to high on one side, warm on the other. Brush one side of a round of dough with olive oil. Pick up the dough with both hands and place, oiled-side down, on the hot side of the grill. Cook until grill marks appear, 2–3 minutes. Flip the dough and arrange the pesto, onions, and 1 oz. (25g) goat's cheese on the cooked side. When the bottom has browned, slide the pizza to the cooler side of the grill. Close the lid and cook the pizza until the toppings are hot and the cheese has melted. Transfer the pizza to a chopping board and continue with the next round of dough. Cut the pizzas and serve immediately.

I sampled this unique combination many years ago at an Italian restaurant in Halifax, Nova Scotia, and have been inspired by it ever since. Ultra-thin sweet potatoes can be achieved with a sharp knife, or better still a mandolin cutter.

Sweet potato, sage, and cambozola

UNIQUE | Makes 1 pizza

- 1 x 12" (30cm) Crispy pizza base (see page 36)
- 1 tsp chili oil
- 5 oz. (150g) cambozola cheese, roughly sliced
- 6 oz. (175g) sweet potato, peeled and thinly sliced
- 4–5 fresh sage leaves, thinly sliced
- Sea salt and freshly ground pepper

Prepare the pizza base so it is ready to be topped. Preheat the oven to 425°F/220°C/gas mark 7.

Spread the base with chili oil, leaving a ½"–¾" (1–2cm) border around the edge. Top with cambozola then the slices of sweet potato. Scatter with sage leaves and season with salt and pepper.

Bake for 10–12 minutes until the crust is golden and the sweet potatoes are cooked through. Serve immediately.

Combining ricotta with basil pesto creates a creamy, rich base for any pizza. Here we've paired it with colorful zucchini (courgettes), fresh from the garden.

Ricotta, pesto, zucchini (courgette), and Parmesan

CREAMY | Makes 1 pizza

> 1 x 12" (30cm) Crispy pizza base (see page 36)
> 5 oz. (150g) ricotta
> 3 Tbsp Basil pesto (see page 178)
> 2 small zucchini (courgettes), thinly sliced (see Tip at right)
> ¾ oz. (20g) Parmesan cheese, grated
> Sea salt and pepper
> 1 small handful fresh parsley leaves, torn

Prepare the pizza base so it is ready to be topped. Preheat the oven to 425°F/220°C/gas mark 7.

Combine the ricotta and pesto in a small bowl. Spread evenly over the base, leaving a ½"–¾" (1–2cm) border around the edge, and top with sliced zucchini (courgette). Sprinkle on the grated Parmesan.

Bake for 10–12 minutes until the crust is golden and the zucchini (courgettes) are slightly curled. Season with sea salt and pepper. Cover with torn parsley leaves. Serve immediately.

Tip: Use a combination of yellow and green zucchini (courgettes) if available.

Blue cheese of any kind elevates pizza to a grown-up level.
Any blue will do, but we love a good Gorgonzola.

Gorgonzola and roasted red onion

SOPHISTICATED | Makes 1 pizza

> 2 large red onions
> 2 Tbsp olive oil
> 2 tsp extra-fine (caster) sugar
> Salt and pepper
> 1 x 12" (30cm) Crispy pizza base (see page 36)
> 9 oz. (250g) Gorgonzola cheese, crumbled
> 1 handful fresh flat-leaf parsley, torn

Preheat the oven to 425°F/220°C/gas mark 7.

Peel the onions and cut each one into 8 wedges. Place them in an oven roasting pan, toss with olive oil and sugar, and season with salt and pepper. Roast the onions in the oven for 30–40 minutes, stirring every 10 minutes, until caramelized. Remove from the heat and leave the oven on at the same temperature.

Prepare the pizza base so it is ready to be topped. Top the base with Gorgonzola and roasted red onions, leaving a ½"–¾" (1–2cm) border around the edge. Bake for 10–12 minutes or until the cheese has melted and the crust is golden. Sprinkle with parsley and serve immediately.

Is it a salad or a pizza? We like to think it's a lovely combination of both.

Tomato pesto, Asiago, and spinach

FRESH | Makes 1 pizza

> 1 x 12" (30cm) Crispy pizza base (see page 36)
> 3½ fl. oz. (100ml) Sun-dried tomato pesto (see page 181)
> 9 oz. (250g) Asiago cheese, grated
> 2 tsp extra virgin olive oil
> 1 tsp balsamic vinegar
> 1 tsp maple syrup or honey
> Sea salt
> 7 oz. (200g) baby spinach, washed and dried (see Tip at right)

Prepare the pizza base so it is ready to be topped. Preheat the oven to 425°F/220°C/gas mark 7.

Spread the pesto evenly over the base, leaving a ½"–¾" (1–2cm) border around the edge. Top with Asiago cheese and bake for 10 minutes until the crust is golden.

Combine the olive oil, balsamic vinegar, maple syrup or honey, and salt to taste. Toss with the spinach and mound on the pizza. Serve immediately.

Tip: Substitute arugula (rocket), watercress, or other greens for the baby spinach.

Roasted eggplant (aubergine), tossed in an intriguing pomegranate molasses vinaigrette, spooned over walnut pesto, and finished with glistening pomegranate seeds, makes for an intensely flavored, divine pizza.

Walnut pesto, eggplant (aubergine), and pomegranate

INTRIGUING | Makes 1 pizza

❯ 1 x 12" (30cm) Crispy pizza base (see page 36)

❯ 3 Tbsp Walnut pesto (see page 180)

❯ 12 oz. (350g) eggplant (aubergine), cut into ¾" (2cm) cubes

❯ 2 Tbsp extra virgin olive oil

❯ 2¼ oz. (60g) crumbled feta cheese

❯ 2 Tbsp pomegranate seeds

FOR THE VINAIGRETTE

❯ 2 Tbsp olive oil

❯ 1 Tbsp pomegranate molasses

❯ 1 tsp clear (runny) honey

❯ ¼ tsp cumin seeds, lightly crushed

Prepare the pizza base so it is ready to be topped. Preheat the oven to 425°F/220°C/gas mark 7.

Prepare the Walnut pesto and set aside. Put the eggplant (aubergine) cubes in an oven roasting pan and toss with olive oil. Roast in the oven for 20 minutes until slightly wilted and discolored. Remove from the heat and keep the oven on at the same temperature. Toss the vinaigrette ingredients in a medium-sized bowl and add the roasted eggplant (aubergine) cubes, tossing to coat.

Spread the Walnut pesto over the base, leaving a ½"–¾" (1–2cm) border around the edge. Spoon the eggplant (aubergine) cubes over the pesto and top with feta. Bake in the middle of the oven for 10–12 minutes until the crust is golden. Remove from the oven, garnish with pomegranate seeds, and serve immediately.

Kids

My childhood Fridays were defined by pizzas. That was when two big pizza pans came out of the cupboard, dough was rolled, sauce was simmered, someone grated the cheese, someone else sliced the toppings, and into the oven it all went. Then the scissors were drawn. Scissors? Yes, the craziest, longest spears of metal a person has ever seen. One quick snip could cut a whole pizza in half.

Friday night pizza at the Camerons isn't an original idea. There are many families out there who reserve Friday night for this familial ritual. It's no wonder—pizzas can be created, one at a time, to suit the picky, sensitive tastebuds of every family member.

Take my sister Lee, for example. By hanging onto the apron strings, Lee could steer and shape her pizza the way she liked it—a huge deal in a family of four daughters. Lee brought Friday night pizzas to her university, where she introduced the ritual to her flatmates. Then, one day, after global travels and many slices of pizza, the moon hit her eye like a big pizza pie—she fell in love with a man whose Friday nights were also devoted to pizza. He even made his own dough.

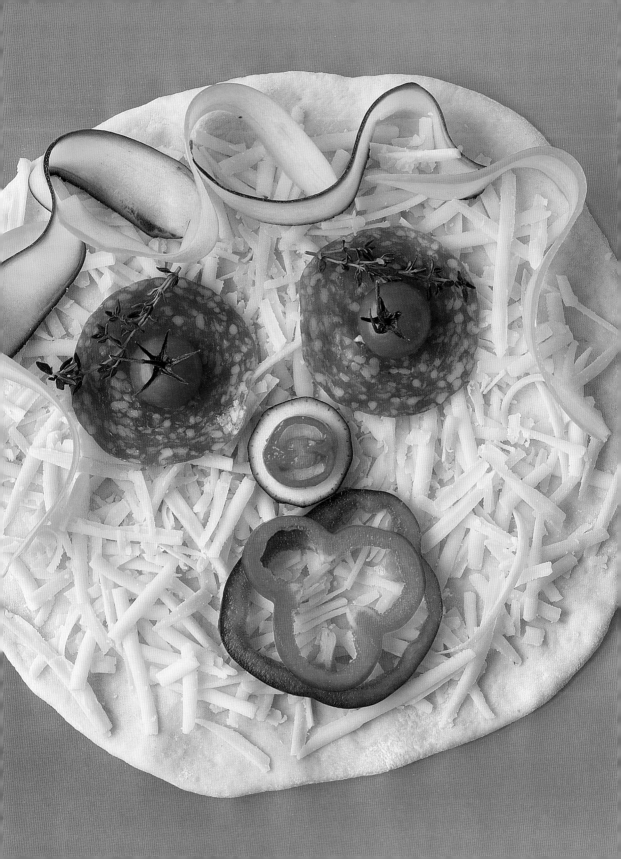

This is a healthy favorite for kids. Sneak in a whole lot of extra goodness by using our Hidden vegetable tomato sauce for kids (see page 186).

Sausage and spinach pizza

COMFORTING | Makes 1 pizza

- 1 x 12" (30cm) Crispy pizza base (see page 36)
- 4 fl. oz. (125ml) Hidden vegetable tomato sauce for kids (see page 186)
- 2-3 sausages of choice (about 7 oz./200g)
- 7 oz. (200g) baby spinach leaves, blanched and well drained
- 5 oz. (150g) mozzarella, sliced

Prepare the pizza base so it is ready to be topped. Preheat the oven to 425°F/220°C/gas mark 7.

Evenly spread the sauce over the base, leaving a ½"–¾" (1-2cm) border around the edge. Squeeze the sausage meat from the casings and evenly scatter on the sauce in small teaspoon-sized amounts. Scatter on the cooked spinach leaves and mozzarella slices.

Cook in the middle of the preheated oven for 10–12 minutes or until crispy and golden. Serve immediately.

This scone-based pizza is more like a bacon and egg pie than a pizza—but then, "pizza" literally means "pie" anyway!

Bacon and egg pizza pie

SUBSTANTIAL | Makes 1 pizza

- 1 x 10" (25cm) Quick scone base (see page 37)
- 2 thin slices bacon, chopped into small cubes
- 1 oz. (30g) grated Cheddar cheese (optional)
- 2 eggs, beaten
- 1 green (spring) onion, finely sliced
- 1 tsp milk
- Salt and freshly ground black pepper

Prepare the Quick scone base by pinching up the edges to form a rim about ½" (1cm) high. Preheat the oven to 400°F/200°C/ gas mark 6.

Evenly scatter the bacon on the base. If using the cheese, scatter it over the bacon at this point. Beat the eggs, green (spring) onion, and milk together in a small bowl and season well with salt and pepper. Pour the egg mixture over the bacon, ensuring it does not spill over the rim.

Put straight into the preheated oven and cook for 12–16 minutes or until the egg has set and the base is cooked. Serve warm or cold.

This is a great pizza for the kids to help make. It requires no rising, so it can go from hand to mouth in 30 minutes! Grating the zucchini (courgettes) will help disguise them and put any vegetable-hater off the scent.

Quick ham, zucchini (courgette), and Cheddar

SIMPLICITY | Makes 1 pizza

- 1 x 10" (25cm) Quick scone base (see page 37)
- 2 fl. oz. (60ml) Quick classic tomato sauce (see page 186)
- 1 zucchini (courgette), grated
- 3 slices ham, chopped into cubes
- 2 oz. (50g) grated Cheddar cheese

Prepare the Quick scone base so it is ready to be topped. Preheat the oven to 400°F/200°C/gas mark 6.

Spread the tomato sauce evenly over the base, leaving a ½" (1cm) border around the edge. Evenly scatter the zucchini (courgette) and ham over the sauce and sprinkle on the grated cheese.

Cook in the middle of the preheated oven for 12–16 minutes or until golden and cooked. Remove from the oven and allow to cool slightly before serving.

These are like a thickened version of Pizza breads (see page 51)
and make a great snack for kids and adults alike!

Pizza fingers

FUN | Makes about 12 fingers

> ½ quantity Focaccia pizza base dough (see page 52)
> Extra virgin olive oil (optional)

TOPPING SUGGESTIONS

> 2 oz. (50g) pepperoni, finely sliced, 1 oz. (30g) Gruyère cheese, and 1 tsp dried oregano

> Brush with 1 Tbsp Pesto (see pages 178–181) combined with 1 Tbsp olive oil and top with 1 oz. (30g) Gruyère cheese

> Brush with 1 Tbsp chili oil and top with 1 oz. (30g) finely grated Gruyère cheese and 1 tsp thyme leaves

> Spread with 2 Tbsp Quick classic tomato sauce (see page 186) and top with 1 oz. (30g) grated Cheddar cheese

> Brush with 1 Tbsp basil oil and sprinkle on sea salt

> Brush with 2 Tbsp melted butter and chopped herbs of your choice

Preheat the oven to 425°F/220°C/gas mark 7. Prepare the Focaccia pizza base dough so it is ready to be shaped. Shape the dough into ovals about 12" (30cm) long and 8" (20cm) wide and place on a lightly floured baking sheet. Make cuts right through the dough, about ¾" (2cm) apart but so they are still attached at the ends, and leave to rest, covered, for 10–15 minutes.

Cover the surface of the dough with your selected toppings and cook for 14–16 minutes or until golden and crispy. Serve straight from the oven, drizzled with extra virgin olive oil, and broken into individual fingers.

Apologies to any vegetarian parents out there, but this pizza was very highly rated at our unofficial kids' pizza taste test. What can we do?

Minced beef, bacon, and mozzarella

SAFE | Makes 1 pizza

- 1 x 12" (30cm) Crispy pizza base (see page 36) or 1 Thick-crust pizza base (see page 38)
- 7 oz. (200g) lean beef, chicken, or turkey mince
- 7 fl. oz. (200ml) Hidden vegetable tomato sauce for kids (see page 186)
- 3 slices bacon, cooked
- 3½ oz. (100g) block mozzarella, grated

Prepare the pizza base so it is ready to be topped. Preheat the oven to 425°F/220°C/gas mark 7.

Heat a heavy-bottomed saucepan over medium heat. Add the mince and cook. When the meat begins to cook, break it up with a wooden spoon. Once cooked, drain off any excess fat. Set aside.

Spoon the sauce over the base, leaving a ½" (1cm) border around the edge. Add the mince. Break the cooked bacon over the pizza. Finish with the grated mozzarella cheese.

Bake in the middle of the oven, 10–12 minutes for a crispy base, 12–15 for a thick crust, until the crust is golden and the cheese is bubbling. Allow to cool slightly, slice, and serve immediately.

A traditional Welsh rarebit usually has beer added to it to make the mixture into more of a paste. I've modified it to be more kid-friendly by adding tomato ketchup instead.

Welsh rarebit and ham pizza

TASTY | Makes 1 pizza

- 1 x 10" (25cm) Quick scone base (see page 37)
- 4 oz. (125g) Cheddar cheese, grated
- 1 onion, grated
- 1–2 tsp Dijon mustard
- 3–4 splashes Worcestershire sauce
- 4 Tbsp tomato ketchup
- 3½ oz. (100g) sliced ham

Prepare the base so it is ready to be topped. Preheat the oven to 400°F/200°C/gas mark 6.

In a bowl, combine the cheese, onion, mustard, Worcestershire sauce, and tomato ketchup until well mixed. Place the ham slices evenly over the base and top with the cheese mixture, spreading it almost to the edges. Cook in the middle of the preheated oven for 16–18 minutes or until lightly golden and the base is cooked. Remove from the oven and allow to cool slightly before eating.

Either of our quick, no-rise doughs, rolled out before a buffet of ingredients, creates the easiest, happiest pizza-making party around.

Make your own pizza party

JOYOUS | Makes 4 x 6" (15cm) pizzas

❭ 1 quantity Quick scone base dough (see page 37) or Gluten-free quick pizza base dough (see page 44)
❭ Quick classic tomato sauce (see page 186)
❭ Store-bought barbecue sauce

ALL, OR A SELECTION, OF THE FOLLOWING TOPPINGS

❭ Hot dogs (frankfurters), chopped into bite-sized pieces
❭ Salami, thinly sliced
❭ Cooked chicken breasts or ham, chopped
❭ 1 green pepper, cored and sliced into rings

❭ 1 red pepper, cored and sliced into rings
❭ 1 small pineapple, chopped into bite-sized pieces
❭ Gouda, harvarti, or Cheddar cheese, grated
❭ Sweet corn
❭ Cherry tomatoes, sliced or halved

Preheat the oven to 425°F/220°C/gas mark 7. Divide the pizza dough into four balls. Roll the balls into 6" (15cm) rounds one at a time on a floured surface. Place the sauces and the topping ingredients in individual bowls.

Allow children to top their own pizzas with their chosen ingredients. Transfer the pizzas to baking sheets lined with baking parchment and bake for 6–8 minutes until the crust is golden and the cheese is bubbling. Allow to cool slightly, slice, and serve.

Isn't it great when fast food is actually healthy?

Hidden vegetable, tomato, and havarti

SIMPLE | Makes 1 pizza

- 1 x 12" (30cm) Crispy pizza base (see page 36) or 1 Gluten-free quick pizza base (see page 44)
- 7 fl. oz. (200ml) Hidden vegetable tomato sauce for kids (see page 186)
- 5 oz. (150g) Cheddar or havarti cheese, cubed
- 2 tomatoes, thinly sliced
- ½ tsp dried oregano

Prepare your chosen pizza base so it is ready to be topped. Preheat the oven to 425°F/220°C/gas mark 7.

Spoon the sauce over the base, leaving a ½" (1cm) border around the edge. Scatter cubed cheese over the sauce. Top with the sliced tomatoes and an even sprinkling of oregano. Bake in the middle of the oven, 10–12 minutes for a crispy base, 12–15 minutes for a gluten-free base, until the crust is golden and the cheese is bubbling. Allow to cool slightly, slice, and serve.

This pizza, which takes its inspiration from the American Southwest, is full of texture and sweet, smoky, and spicy flavors. Leftover ham is perfect for this pizza—the tastier the ham, the better the pizza! Store-bought barbecue sauce can be used if you are short on time.

Sweet corn, ham, and red pepper

SMOKY | Makes 1 pizza

- 1 x 12″ (30cm) Crispy pizza base (see page 36) or 1 Thick-crust pizza base (see page 38)
- 2 Tbsp Mustard bourbon barbecue sauce (see page 187)
- 6 oz. (175g) cooked ham, torn into bite-size pieces
- 3 oz. (80g) sweet corn
- 1 small red pepper, seeded and cubed
- 2¾ oz. (75g) smoked Gouda cheese, grated
- Handful fresh cilantro leaves (coriander), to garnish (optional)

Prepare the pizza base so it is ready to be topped. Preheat the oven to 425°F/220°C/gas mark 7.

Spoon the barbecue sauce over the base, leaving a ½" (1cm) border around the edge. Top with the ham, sweet corn, and pepper. Finish with grated cheese. Bake for 10–12 minutes for a crispy crust, 12–15 minutes for a thick crust, until the crust is golden. Garnish with cilantro (coriander), if using, and serve immediately.

Sweet

My goddaughter, Little Lindsay, has tasted-tested more of my recipes than she would care to remember. She's sampled fiery spices, savory ice creams, dark green juices, nutty burgers, and pizzas, both barbecued and baked. She tastes, she swallows, and she is always honest. But little Lindsay draws the line at chocolate pizza. I wonder what she's thinking. *Is that meat simmering on the stove about to be spooned over a chocolate pizza? What about the mound of grated smoked Gouda cheese? Will I have to eat it?*

Not to worry, little Lindsay. This chapter is all about sweetness. Sweetened dough, sweetened topping, sweetened syrups. There may be nuts in some of the recipes, a little coconut, perhaps even a splash of sweet wine. But no meat.

Sweetness is the essence of this chapter. We've taken the traditional pizza shape and applied our favorite sweet flavors to the formula. And besides, doesn't everyone want a triangular-shaped portion of dessert?

This pizza uses grapes at several different stages in their production. They seem to just get sweeter and sweeter.

Grape, raisin, and vin santo

VITICULTURE | Makes 1 pizza

- 2¾ oz. (75g) raisins
- 2 fl. oz. (50ml) vin santo or Marsala
- 1 x 12″ (30cm) thick crust Sweet honey pizza base (see page 53)
- 7 oz. (200g) seedless red and black grapes
- 1–2 Tbsp dark brown (demerara) sugar
- Mascarpone or crème fraîche, to serve (optional)

Soak the raisins in the vin santo or Marsala overnight.

Prepare the pizza base so it is ready to be topped. Preheat the oven to 425°F/220°C/gas mark 7.

Evenly scatter the soaked raisins and grapes over the base, leaving a ½″–¾″ (1–2cm) border around the edge. Sprinkle on the sugar and drizzle on any extra vin santo that was not absorbed by the raisins.

Cook in the middle of the preheated oven for 10–12 minutes or until golden and crispy. Remove from the oven and serve immediately. Add a dollop of mascarpone or crème fraîche on the top of each slice, if desired.

This pizza is really on the borderline between sweet and savory. To go the more savory way, omit the honey and add a handful of arugula (rocket) leaves and a good grind of black pepper just before serving.

Fig, rosemary, and blue cheese

FRAGRANT | Makes 1 pizza

- 2 Tbsp extra virgin olive oil
- 1 red onion, finely sliced
- 1 tsp finely chopped fresh rosemary
- 5 fl. oz. (150ml) red wine
- 3½ fl. oz. (100ml) balsamic vinegar
- 2 oz. (50g) extra-fine (caster) sugar
- 5 oz. (150g) plump dried figs, quartered
- 1 x 12″ (30cm) Crispy pizza base (see page 36)
- 3½ oz. (100g) Gorgonzola, dolcelatte, or Stilton cheese

Heat the oil in a nonstick frying pan or sauté pan. Add the onions and sauté until soft but not browned, about 6–8 minutes. Add the rosemary and sauté for 1 more minute before adding the wine and vinegar. Keep the heat at medium until the liquid has reduced by half. Add the sugar and figs and reduce the heat. Cook, stirring occasionally, for 15–20 minutes or until the mixture is the consistency of a syrupy jam. Remove from the heat and cool.

Preheat the oven to 425°F/220°C/gas mark 7. Prepare the pizza base so it is ready to be topped. Spread the fig and rosemary preserve over the base, leaving a ½″–¾″ (1–2cm) border around the edge. Evenly scatter on chunks of the blue cheese.

Cook in the middle of the preheated oven for 10–12 minutes or until crispy and golden. Serve immediately.

Serve this pizza with a few basil leaves scattered on top and a glass of sweet dessert wine. This is a favorite combination of ours.

Pear, pecorino, and walnut

SAVORY-SWEET | Makes 1 pizza

- 1 x 12" (30cm) Crispy pizza base (see page 36)
- 1 Tbsp basil or lemon oil (plain oil will do if you don't have any)
- 1 pear, cored and cut into slices (see Tip at right)
- 2 oz. (50g) pecorino cheese, thinly shaved
- 2 oz. (50g) walnut pieces
- Freshly ground black pepper
- 1 Tbsp clear (runny) honey, to serve

Prepare the pizza base so it is ready to be topped. Preheat the oven to 425°F/220°C/gas mark 7.

Brush the basil oil, using a pastry brush, all over the base. Scatter on the pear slices or fan them if you have time, leaving a ½"–¾" (1–2cm) border around the edge. Then scatter on the pecorino cheese and the walnut pieces. Season lightly with black pepper. Cook in the middle of the preheated oven for 10–12 minutes or until crispy and golden. Drizzle on the honey and serve immediately.

Tip: Bosc pears—large, slender pears with rust-colored skin—hold their shape well when baked. Any pear, however, will do. Increase the quantity if the pears are small.

This is the ultimate decadent dessert.

Banana, chocolate, and pecan

INDULGENT | Makes 1 pizza

- 4½ oz. (130g) butter
- 4 oz. (120g) 70% dark chocolate (continental plain baking chocolate), chopped
- 4 eggs
- ¼ tsp salt
- 10 oz. (300g) extra-fine (caster) sugar
- 1 tsp vanilla extract
- 6 oz. (170g) plain flour

FOR THE TOPPING
- 1 banana
- Juice of 1 lemon
- 3½ fl. oz. (100ml) sour cream or mascarpone
- ¼ tsp nutmeg
- 12–15 pecan nuts
- 1 Tbsp dark brown (demerara) sugar

Preheat the oven to 350°F/180°C/gas mark 4. Put the butter and chocolate in a heatproof bowl set over a pan of simmering water. Stir occasionally until melted. Set aside to cool. Beat the eggs with the salt in an electric mixer until pale. Slowly add the extra-fine (caster) sugar with the beaters going until the mixture is light and fluffy. Stir in the vanilla and the chocolate mixture and beat until smooth. Fold in the flour until combined.

Put the banana, lemon juice, sour cream, and nutmeg in a bowl and mash together.

Line a 14" x 16" (36 x 41cm) baking sheet with baking parchment. Spoon the chocolate mixture onto the parchment and spread into a 12" (30cm) circle. Using a teaspoon, randomly spoon the banana mixture over the chocolate pizza base, as if topping a pizza. Press the topping gently into the base. Scatter on the pecans and dark brown (demerara) sugar.

Bake in the center of the oven for 25 minutes until cooked through in the center, but still very moist. Cool, slice, and serve.

This festive, colorfully sweet pizza is delicious with a glass of white wine and a sampling of cheeses.

Cranberry, orange, and mascarpone

FESTIVE | Makes 1 pizza

- 1 x 12" (30cm) thick crust Sweet honey pizza base (see page 53), with the saffron omitted and substituting orange rind for the lemon
- 10 oz. (300g) cranberries, fresh or frozen
- 2½ fl. oz. (75ml) orange juice
- 3½ oz. (100g) extra-fine (caster) sugar
- 2 Tbsp walnuts, chopped
- 7 oz. (200g) mascarpone

Preheat the oven to 400°F/200°C/gas mark 6. Prepare the pizza base so it is ready for topping and set aside.

Put the cranberries in a medium-sized saucepan over medium heat. Add the orange juice and sugar, stir, and simmer the berries for 10–12 minutes until they begin to pop (let them simmer a few minutes longer if using frozen cranberries). Remove the pan from the heat. Stir in the walnuts and 3½ oz. (100g) mascarpone into the cranberry mixture. Spoon the rest of the mascarpone over the pizza base. Top with the cranberry mixture.

Bake for 12 minutes until the crust is golden and cooked through. Cool slightly, slice, and serve.

Is it a calzone or an apple turnover?
You could be forgiven for thinking either.

Apple, sultana, and cinnamon strudel

SPICED | Makes 2 pizza strudels

- ½ quantity Sweet honey pizza base dough (see page 53)
- 2–3 (about 1 lb. 2 oz./500g) apples, peeled, cored, and sliced
- Juice of 1 lemon
- 4 Tbsp sultanas
- 2 Tbsp brandy
- 1 tsp cinnamon
- ½ tsp ground nutmeg
- 2 Tbsp extra-fine (caster) sugar (optional)
- 2 Tbsp melted butter
- 2 Tbsp brown sugar
- Crème fraîche, to serve

Preheat the oven to 425°F/220°C/gas mark 7. Divide the dough into two and roll each out into 12" (30cm) rounds on baking parchment. Leave to rest for about 10 minutes.

In a bowl, combine the apple slices, lemon juice, sultanas, brandy, cinnamon, ground nutmeg, and sugar, if using, and mix to combine. Leave to rest for about 5 minutes, then drain and scatter the apple slices and sultanas over one half of the base, leaving ¾" (2cm) as a rim. Pull the uncovered half of base up and over the filling and, using your fingers, crimp the edge to seal it, forming a crescent shape. Prick the top once or twice with a fork, brush with the melted butter, and sprinkle on the brown sugar.

Carefully transfer the baking parchment to a baking sheet and cook for about 15 minutes or until golden and the base is cooked through. Allow to rest for a few minutes before serving with crème fraîche.

It's a wonderful thing when favorite flavors come together in one perfect circle.

Chocolate brownie

DECADENT | Makes 1 pizza

⟩ 4½ oz. (130g) butter
⟩ 4 oz. (120g) 70% dark chocolate (continental plain baking chocolate), chopped
⟩ 4 eggs
⟩ ¼ tsp salt
⟩ 10 oz. (300g) extra-fine (caster) sugar
⟩ 1 tsp vanilla extract
⟩ 6 oz. (170g) plain flour

FOR THE TOPPING
⟩ 5 oz. (150g) cream cheese, at room temperature
⟩ 2 oz. (50g) sweet desiccated coconut
⟩ 2 oz. (50g) chocolate chips, or plain chocolate, roughly chopped

Preheat the oven to 350°F/180°C/gas mark 4. Put the butter and chocolate in a heatproof bowl set over a pan of simmering water. Stir occasionally until melted. Set aside to cool.

Beat the eggs with the salt in an electric mixer until pale. Slowly add the sugar with the beaters going until the mixture is light and fluffy. Stir in the vanilla and the chocolate mixture and beat until smooth. Fold in the flour until combined.

Put the cream cheese, coconut, and chocolate chips in a bowl. Mash the mixture with a fork until combined.

Line a 14" x 16" (36 x 41cm) baking sheet with baking parchment. Spoon the chocolate mixture onto the parchment and spread into a 12" (30cm) circle. Using a teaspoon, randomly spoon the cream cheese mixture over the chocolate pizza base, as if topping a pizza. Press the topping lightly into the chocolate base. Bake in the center of the oven for 25 minutes until the center is cooked but still very moist. Cool, slice, and serve.

Tarte tatin, the classic French upside-down tart, is traditionally made with caramelized apples and topped with puff pastry and baked in the oven. Here, the tarte tatin enters the pizza world featuring pears, cranberries, and pecans all caramelized together with a sweet pizza crust. It's the perfect festive brunch fare.

Pear pizza tatin

COMFORT | Makes 1 pizza

- 1 thin crust Sweet honey pizza base (see page 53), with the saffron omitted
- 1 lb. 10 oz. (800g) pears, peeled, cored, and quartered
- ½ tsp Chinese five-spice powder
- 4½ oz. (130g) extra-fine (caster) sugar
- 2 Tbsp butter
- 2 Tbsp cranberries (optional)
- Handful pecans

Preheat the oven to 350°F/180°C/gas mark 4. Prepare the pizza base, rolling it out to approximately 10" (25cm) in diameter, and set aside.

In a large bowl, toss the pear quarters with the Chinese five-spice powder. Put the sugar in a 9½" (24cm) diameter, 1¾" (4.5cm) deep ovenproof frying pan. Scatter the butter over the sugar. Arrange pears in a snug circle around the pan, cut sides facing in the same direction. Tuck the remaining pears inside the circle. Scatter the cranberries and pecans between the pears. Heat the pan over medium to medium-high heat. Juices will bubble. Continue to cook, shaking the pan to loosen the contents every so often, until the juices have caramelized to a dark golden color, about 30 minutes. Watch carefully so it doesn't burn. Remove from the heat but leave contents in the pan.

Place the pizza base over the pears in the pan, tucking the edges of the base inside the pan. Bake for 10 minutes, cover with foil, and bake for 15 more minutes. Invert the pan onto a serving platter. Cool slightly, slice, and serve.

Sauces and more

PESTO

Pesto was invented by the Genoese as a vehicle for the abundant and loved herb, basil. Traditionally it was made from olive oil, garlic, pine nuts, butter, and grated Parmesan cheese. These days pesto has taken on a whole new meaning and covers a whole range of sauces acting as a vehicle for one dominant ingredient, such as walnuts, arugula (rocket), or red peppers. On pages 178–181 are a few of our favorite interpretations of pesto.

Basil pesto

Makes 8 fl. oz. (250ml)

> 1 large bunch (about 2¼–3 oz./60–80g) basil, leaves only
> 2 cloves garlic, peeled and chopped
> 2 oz. (50g) finely grated Parmesan cheese
> 2 oz. (50g) pine nuts
> About 5–7 fl. oz. (150–200ml) extra virgin olive oil

Put the basil, garlic, Parmesan, and pine nuts and a good splash of the olive oil in a food processor and mix until blended. With the motor still running, slowly add the remaining olive oil through the feed tube until the desired consistency is reached. Transfer to a jar or airtight container and cover with a thin layer of oil. Seal and refrigerate for up to 2 weeks.

Parsley pesto

Makes 8 fl. oz. (250ml)

- 1 large bunch (about 2¼–3 oz./60–80g) flat-leaf parsley
- 1 clove garlic, peeled and roughly chopped
- 2 oz. (50g) finely grated Parmesan cheese
- 2 oz. (50g) pine nuts
- Grated rind of 1 lemon
- About 5–7 fl. oz. (150–200ml) extra virgin olive oil
- Salt and freshly ground black pepper to taste

Put the parsley, garlic, Parmesan, pine nuts, and lemon rind in a food processor with about a quarter of the olive oil. Mix to a coarse purée. With the motor still running, drizzle in the remaining olive oil until the desired consistency is reached. Season the pesto with salt and pepper. Parmesan cheese varies in saltiness, so it is important to taste the pesto first before seasoning. Transfer to a jar or airtight container and cover with a thin layer of oil. Seal and refrigerate for up to 2 weeks.

Arugula (rocket) pesto

Makes 8 fl. oz. (250ml)

- 2¼–3 oz. (60–80g) arugula (rocket) leaves
- 1 clove garlic, crushed
- 2 oz. (50g) finely grated Parmesan cheese
- 2 oz. (50g) pine nuts
- 7 fl. oz. (150–200ml) extra virgin olive oil
- Sea salt and freshly ground black pepper to taste

Put the arugula (rocket), garlic, Parmesan, and pine nuts in a food processor with about a quarter of the olive oil. Mix to a coarse purée. With the motor still running, drizzle in the remaining olive oil until the desired consistency is reached. Season the pesto with salt and pepper. Parmesan varies in saltiness, so it is important to taste the pesto before seasoning. Transfer to an airtight container and cover with a thin layer of oil. Seal and refrigerate for up to 2 weeks.

Walnut pesto

Makes 8 fl. oz. (250ml)

- 2 cloves garlic, peeled and roughly chopped
- 2 oz. (50g) grated Parmesan cheese
- 3½ oz. (100g) fresh shelled walnuts
- 4–5 fl. oz. (125–150ml) extra virgin olive oil
- 1 handful basil leaves, torn
- Salt and freshly ground black pepper to taste

Put the garlic, Parmesan, walnuts, and a good splash of olive oil in a food processor and mix to a paste. With the motor still running, drizzle in the remaining olive oil until the desired consistency is reached. Tear up the basil into the food processor and pulse once or twice to combine, but do not mix to completely purée the basil. Add salt and pepper. Transfer to a jar or airtight container and cover with a thin layer of olive oil. Seal and refrigerate for up to 2 weeks.

Cilantro (coriander) pesto

Makes 8 fl. oz. (250ml)

- 2 cloves garlic, peeled and roughly chopped
- 3 Tbsp grated Parmesan cheese
- 1 oz. (25g) freshly shelled walnuts
- 1 red chili, halved, with stem and seeds removed
- 2½ fl. oz. (75ml) extra virgin olive oil
- 1½ oz. (40g) cilantro leaves (coriander)
- ½ oz. (10g) mint
- ¼ oz. (10g) chives
- Grated rind of 1 lime
- Juice of ½ lime
- Salt and freshly ground black pepper to taste

Put the garlic, Parmesan, walnuts, chili, and 1 Tbsp of the olive oil in a food processor and mix to a paste. With the motor still running, drizzle in the remaining olive oil until the desired consistency is reached. Add the herbs, lime rind, and juice to the food processor and pulse to combine, but do not mix to completely purée the herbs. Add salt and pepper to taste. Transfer to a jar or airtight container and cover with a thin layer of oil. Seal and refrigerate for up to 2 weeks.

Roasted red pepper and olive pesto

Makes 8 fl. oz. (250ml)

- 1½ oz. (40g) sun-dried tomatoes, (dry, not packed in oil)
- 1 small red pepper, roasted, peeled, deseeded, and roughly chopped
- 5 kalamata olives, pitted and roughly chopped
- ⅛ oz. (5g) flat-leaf parsley
- ⅛ oz. (5g) basil
- ¾ oz. (20g) grated Parmesan cheese
- 2 cloves garlic, crushed
- 2 Tbsp extra virgin olive oil
- ½ tsp balsamic vinegar
- Sea salt and ground black pepper to taste

Put the sun-dried tomatoes in a small bowl and cover with boiling water. Leave to soften for 20 minutes. Drain water, pushing as much liquid from the tomatoes as possible. Place them in a food processor with the chopped red pepper, olives, parsley, basil, Parmesan, and garlic. Pulse until the mixture is roughly chopped. Add the olive oil and balsamic vinegar and continue to pulse until coarse but spreadable. Add salt and pepper to taste. Cover the pesto with a thin layer of olive oil. Seal and refrigerate for up to 2 weeks.

Sun-dried tomato pesto

Makes 4 fl. oz. (125ml)

- 1¼ oz. (30g) sun-dried tomatoes
- 2½ fl. oz. (75ml) red wine vinegar
- 2 fl. oz. (50ml) balsamic vinegar
- 3 cloves garlic, crushed
- 1 tsp extra-fine (caster) sugar
- 2½ fl. oz. (75ml) extra virgin olive oil
- Sea salt and pepper to taste

Place the sun-dried tomatoes and both vinegars in a small saucepan and bring to a gentle simmer. Remove from the heat and allow to sit for 5 minutes until the tomatoes are slightly softened. Pour the tomatoes and vinegars into a food processor. Add the garlic, sugar, and olive oil and pulse until roughly blended. Add salt and pepper to taste. Use immediately or transfer to a jar or airtight container and cover with a thin layer of olive oil. Seal and refrigerate for up to 2 weeks.

Slow-roasted tomatoes

Makes enough for 1–2 pizzas

The intense flavor of the tomatoes becomes very concentrated after long, slow cooking. When tomatoes are in season, you may not even need to add any sugar. Make more than you need and preserve them in oil until needed.

> 1 lb. 12 oz. (800g) medium-sized plum tomatoes
> 1 Tbsp extra virgin olive oil
> 1 tsp extra-fine (caster) sugar
> ½ tsp dried oregano

Preheat the oven to 250°F/120°C/gas mark ½. Cut the tomatoes in half lengthways and scoop out the seeds. Place the tomatoes, cut side up, on a baking sheet and drizzle on the oil. Evenly sprinkle on the sugar and oregano and put in the oven. Roast the tomatoes for 2–2½ hours or until semi-dried. Remove from the oven, cool, and store in an airtight container for 3–4 days in the fridge. Alternatively, cover completely in extra virgin olive oil, seal in a sterilized jar, and keep for up to 2 months.

Slow-roasted tomato sauce

Makes enough for 1–2 pizzas

- 1 quantity Slow-roasted tomatoes (see page 182)
- Handful basil leaves
- 1–2 cloves garlic, roughly chopped
- 2 Tbsp extra virgin olive oil

Put the roasted tomatoes in a food processor or, alternatively, grind by hand using a mortar and pestle. Add the basil leaves, garlic, and olive oil. Pulse or grind to a coarse paste. This sauce can be stored in the fridge in an airtight container for up to 1 week.

Sweet cherry tomato sauce

Makes enough for 2 pizzas

- 1 lb. 12 oz. (800g) cherry tomatoes, halved
- 2 cloves garlic, sliced
- 2 sprigs rosemary, leaves only
- 1 Tbsp clear (runny) honey
- 1 Tbsp extra virgin olive oil
- Sea salt and freshly ground black pepper to taste

Preheat the oven to 400°F/200°C/gas mark 6. Place the tomatoes, cut side up, on a baking sheet. Sprinkle on the garlic slices and rosemary leaves, then evenly drizzle on the honey and oil. Season with salt and pepper and roast in the oven for 10–12 minutes or until the tomatoes are bursting and juicy. Allow to cool before tipping the tomatoes and all the juices into an airtight container. This sauce can be refrigerated in an airtight container for up to 3–4 days.

Spicy tomato sauce

Makes 1¼ pint (650ml)

Remove the chili flakes for a more classic, concentrated, cooked tomato sauce.

› 2 Tbsp olive oil
› 1 large onion, finely chopped
› 3 cloves garlic, peeled
› 1 tsp dried oregano

› ½–1 tsp dried chili flakes
› 2 x 14 oz. (400g) cans chopped tomatoes

Heat the oil in a large saucepan. Add the onion and sauté for 2–3 minutes or until translucent but not browned. Add the garlic, oregano, and chili flakes and sauté for 1–2 more minutes, stirring occasionally. Add the canned tomatoes and bring to a boil, stirring. Reduce the heat and simmer for about 25 minutes or until richly red and concentrated, stirring occasionally. Allow to cool and store in the fridge, in an airtight container, for up to 1 week.

Tomato and roasted red pepper sauce

Makes 18 fl. oz. (500ml)—enough for 4 pizzas

This pizza sauce is based on a Croatian sauce called Ajvar. My friend Sarah Carlyle and I managed to add it to every meal as we camped our way along the Croatian coast. I've invented my own version and decided it is just as suited to pizza.

› 3 large red peppers, halved and deseeded
› 1 lb. 5 oz. (600g) tomatoes, halved

› ¼–½ tsp dried chili flakes
› 2 cloves garlic, sliced
› 2 Tbsp extra virgin olive oil

Preheat the oven to 400°F/200°C/gas mark 6. Place the red pepper, cut side down, on a baking sheet and roast for about 25–30 minutes or until starting to blacken. Put the tomatoes, cut side up, on a separate sheet and sprinkle on the dried chili flakes and garlic slices, then drizzle on the olive oil. Add to the oven about 10 minutes after the peppers and roast for 15–20 minutes. When the peppers are ready, remove from the oven and leave until cool enough to handle. Peel off the skin and put the flesh in a food processor. Add the tomatoes and all the juices and process in bursts until blended but not too smooth. Allow to cool, then store in the fridge, in an airtight container, for up to 1 week.

Black olive tapénade

Makes 8 fl. oz. (250ml)

> 6 oz. (170g) pitted black olives, drained
> 2 oz. (50g) anchovy fillets
> 2 Tbsp capers, rinsed
> 2 fl. oz. (50ml) extra virgin olive oil
> Freshly ground black pepper to taste

Put the olives, anchovies, and capers in the bowl of a food processor and pulse to combine. With the motor running, pour in the oil through the feed tube. Season to taste with freshly ground black pepper. Transfer to a jar, cover with a thin layer of oil, and refrigerate for up to 2 weeks.

Caramelized fennel relish

Makes enough for 1–2 pizzas

> 1 Tbsp extra virgin olive oil
> 1 onion, thinly sliced
> 1 large bulb fennel, very thinly sliced
> 1 clove garlic, crushed
> 4 Tbsp extra-fine (caster) sugar
> 1 Tbsp whole-grain mustard
> 2 Tbsp white wine vinegar or cider vinegar
> Salt and freshly ground black pepper to taste

Heat the oil in a nonstick saucepan over medium heat and add the onion, fennel, and garlic. Stir until well coated in the oil and the onion and fennel start to soften but not brown. Increase the heat, add the sugar, and stir constantly for 2–3 more minutes or until starting to brown. Stir in the mustard and vinegar and season generously with salt and pepper. When the liquid has evaporated, reduce the heat slightly and leave the mixture to caramelize and darken around the edges, stirring occasionally, for 8–12 more minutes. Set aside to cool. This relish can be made up to 3 days in advance and kept for up to 1 week stored in an airtight container in the fridge.

Quick classic tomato sauce

Makes 18 fl. oz. (500ml)

This is an excellent sauce to have on hand—it takes seconds to make and keeps for up to 1 week in the fridge or up to 3 months in the freezer. Experiment with the amount of spice to suit your taste.

- 1¼ pint (796ml) canned tomatoes, well drained
- 3 Tbsp tomato purée
- 1 tsp dried basil
- 1 tsp dried oregano
- ½ tsp extra-fine (caster) sugar
- ½ tsp salt
- ½ tsp dried chili flakes
- ½ tsp crushed black pepper
- 2 cloves garlic, finely chopped (optional)

Combine all ingredients in a food processor and blend until smooth. Transfer to a small bowl and use immediately, or cover and either refrigerate for up to 1 week or freeze.

Hidden vegetable tomato sauce for kids

Makes 1¾ pint (1L)

This mild-flavored sauce is the perfect way to pack nutrients into your children's pizza. Spoon it over a base, top with cheese, and voilà, a healthy, simple meal.

- 1 lb. 12 oz. (800g) canned tomatoes, drained
- 5 oz. (150g) zucchini (courgettes), roughly chopped
- 5 oz. (150g) carrots, peeled and roughly chopped
- 7 oz. (200g) baby spinach
- 7 oz. (200g) onion, peeled and roughly chopped
- 2 cloves garlic, crushed
- ½ tsp salt

Combine all the ingredients in a food processor and blend until roughly chopped. (Take it further if you think the vegetables are too visible!) Pour the sauce into a large saucepan and simmer, uncovered, for 40 minutes, stirring frequently, until the sauce has reduced by half. Use 5–7 fl. oz. (150–200ml) of sauce for a 12" (30cm) pizza. Freeze any remaining sauce in an airtight container for up to 6 months.

Caramelized onions

Makes enough for 2–3 pizzas

> 1 Tbsp olive oil
> 1 Tbsp butter
> 2 large onions, thinly sliced
> Salt and freshly ground pepper to taste
> ½ tsp anchovy paste (optional)

Heat the olive oil and butter in a large frying pan over medium-high heat. Add the onions and reduce the heat to low. Sauté until softened, stirring occasionally. Add a sprinkling of salt and pepper, but not too much salt, as the anchovy paste will add a salty kick. Continue to sauté over low heat, stirring occasionally, until brown and caramelized, 20–30 minutes. Mix in the anchovy paste (if using), stir, and remove from heat. These onions can be kept in the fridge for up to 1 week.

Mustard bourbon barbecue sauce

Makes 1¼ pint (750ml)

It doesn't get much better than this rich, sweet yet smoky, decadent sauce. The sauce will keep, covered, for up to 3 weeks in the fridge, or store it in an airtight container in the freezer for up to 6 months.

> 1 tsp vegetable oil
> 1 bunch green (spring) onions, chopped
> 1 medium white onion, chopped
> 4 large cloves garlic, chopped
> 7 oz. (200g) packed golden brown sugar
> 4 fl. oz. (125ml) tomato ketchup
> 2½ fl. oz. (75ml) tomato purée
> 4 fl. oz. (125ml) whole-grain Dijon mustard
> 4 fl. oz. (125ml) water
> 2½ fl. oz. (75ml) Worcestershire sauce
> 2½ fl. oz. (75ml) cider vinegar
> 2½ fl. oz. (75ml) apple juice
> 1 chipotle chili in adobo sauce, finely chopped
> 1 tsp ground cumin
> 12 fl. oz. (350ml) bourbon or whisky
> Salt and freshly ground black pepper to taste

Heat the oil in a heavy, large pan over medium-low heat. Add the green (spring) onions, white onion, and garlic and sauté until tender, about 15 minutes. Mix in the remaining ingredients, adding the bourbon last. Simmer the sauce until thick and reduced to 1¼ pint (750ml), stirring occasionally, for about 1 hour. Season to taste with salt and pepper. This sauce can be prepared 2 weeks in advance. Cover and refrigerate.

About the authors

New Zealander Pippa Cuthbert (right) has a background in Food Science and Human Nutrition from Otago University in New Zealand. After starting her career working in the test kitchen of Nestlé New Zealand, Pippa moved to London, where she met Lindsay. Pippa spent nine years in London building a successful career as a Food Writer and Food Stylist and discovered a passion for wood-fired pizza while working on cookery courses in Tuscany with cookbook author Ursula Ferrigno. Pippa returned home to New Zealand in 2009, where she now lives with her husband and three young children. She continues to work on a freelance basis doing food writing and food styling for editorial, advertising, packaging, and TVCs.

Lindsay Cameron Wilson (left) is a food writer, recipe developer, and host of *The Food Podcast*. She met Pippa while working at Books for Cooks in London, where their cookbook collaboration began. Pippa's a New Zealander; Lindsay is Canadian. Together they've created seven cookbooks that celebrate the flavors of their homes and all the adventures in between. Lindsay lives on the east coast of Canada with her husband and three boys, where a pizza paddle is never far away.

Bibliography

Amandonico, Nikko. *La Pizza*. Mitchell Beazley, 2001.
David, Elizabeth. *English Bread and Yeast Cookery*. Penguin, 2001.
——. *Italian Food*. Penguin, 1963.
Ferrigno, Ursula, and Eric Trieulle. *Bread*. Dorling Kindersley, 1988.
Harzan, Marcella. *The Essentials of Classic Italian Cooking*. Macmillan, 1992.
McGee, Harold. *On Food and Cooking*. Simon & Schuster Inc., 1984.
Steingarten, Jeffrey. *It Must've Been Something I Ate*. Vintage Books, 2003.

List of recipes

Index